OFFICE 2003

STEPHEN COPESTAKE

in easy steps

In easy steps is an imprint of Computer Step
Southfield Road . Southam
Warwickshire CV47 0FB . United Kingdom
www.ineasysteps.com

Notice of Liability
Every effort has been made to ensure that this book contains accurate and current information. However, Computer Step and the author shall not be liable for any loss or damage suffered by readers as a result of any information contained herein.

Trademarks
Microsoft® and Windows® are registered trademarks of Microsoft Corporation. All other trademarks are acknowledged as belonging to their respective companies.

Printed and bound in the United Kingdom

ISBN-13 978-1-84078-264-6
ISBN-10 1-84078-264-1

Table of Contents

Excel 2003 99

Outlook 2003 143

PowerPoint 2003 159

Access 2003 189

Mail merging 225

Index 233

Getting started

This chapter will get you up-and-running in any Office 2003 module. You'll quickly create new documents and open/save existing ones, including to FTP and Internet sites. You'll go on to use Office Online to get help with problems and access to lots of great "added-value" features. You'll also get answers to questions via each module's inbuilt HELP system.

Finally, you'll enhance your use of Office with additional suite-wide features. These include saving configuration settings, Quick File Switching, error repair and copying/pasting multiple items via the Office Clipboard.

Covers

Chapter One

Introduction

Microsoft Office 2003 consists of these principal modules:

- Word 2003 – word-processor

- Excel 2003 – spreadsheet

- Outlook 2003 – personal/business information manager

- PowerPoint 2003 – presentation/slide show creator

- Access 2003 – database

You can target Web output at specific browsers. In any module apart from Access and Outlook, pull down the Tools menu and click Options. In the Options dialog, select the General tab and click Web Options. In the Web Options dialog, select the Browsers tab. Select a browser/version and click OK twice.

Four at least of these programs are leaders in their respective fields. The point about Office, however, is that it integrates its modules exceptionally well. With the exception of Outlook, which has to adopt a relatively individualistic approach, the modules share a common look and feel. (See Chapter 7 for a specific way to integrate the Office modules.)

The illustration below shows the Word opening screen. Flagged are components which are also common to PowerPoint, Access, Outlook and Excel. (There are also differences between the module screens: Outlook, for instance, because of its very different nature, has fewer toolbars. We'll explore this in later chapters.)

Microsoft continually supplies updates and patches for Office. Check regularly on http://office. microsoft.com/officeupdate/.

Title bar   Menu bar   Toolbar

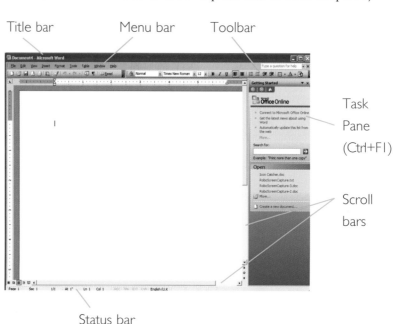

Task Pane (Ctrl+F1)

Scroll bars

Status bar

Toolbars

To add a new button to a toolbar, right-click over the toolbar. Click Customize. In the dialog which launches, click the Commands tab. In the Categories field, click a category (a group of associated icons). In the Commands box, drag a button onto the toolbar in the open document. Click Close.

You can create your own toolbar. In the Customize dialog (see the above tip), select the Toolbars tab and hit New. Name the toolbar and allocate a template.

You can't rename any of the toolbars that come with Office.

The Task Pane is a toolbar. To hide or show it, uncheck or check the Task Pane entry on the right.

Toolbars are important components in all five Office 2003 modules. A toolbar is an on-screen bar which contains shortcut buttons. These symbolize and allow easy access to often-used commands which would normally have to be invoked via one or more menus.

For example, Word 2003's Standard toolbar lets you:

- create, open, save and print documents

- perform copy & paste and cut & paste operations

- undo editing actions

- insert a hyperlink

by simply clicking on the relevant button.

Toolbars vary to some extent from module to module. We'll be looking at these in more detail as we encounter them. For the moment, some general advice:

Specifying which toolbars are displayed
In any Office module, pull down the View menu and click Toolbars. Now do the following:

1 This is Word's toolbar list. Available toolbars in the other Office 2003 programs vary slightly

2 Check the toolbar you want to be visible

Repeat this procedure for as many toolbars as necessary.

Automatic customization

Menus and toolbars are personalized in Office 2003 modules.

Submenus aren't customized.

Personalized menus

When you first use a module, its menus display the features which Microsoft believes are used 95% of the time and features which are infrequently used are not immediately visible. This makes for less cluttered screens.

Personalizing menus is made clear in the illustrations below:

Office 2003 menus expand automatically, after a slight delay. However, to expand them manually, click the chevrons at the bottom of the menu.

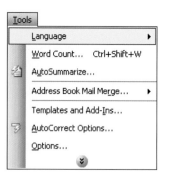

Word 2003's Tools menu, as it first appears...

Automatic customization also applies to toolbars. Note the following:

- *if possible, they display on a single row*
- *they overlap when there isn't enough room on-screen*
- *icons are "promoted" and "demoted" like menu entries*
- *demoted icons are shown in a separate fly-out, reached by clicking:*

...the expanded menu. (As you use the modules, individual features are dynamically promoted or demoted. This means menus are continually evolving)

Creating new documents

Because Word 2003, PowerPoint 2003, Excel 2003 and Access 2003 are more or less uniform in the way they create new documents, we'll look at this topic here rather than in later chapters that are specific to each program.

(However, see Chapter 5 for specialized advice on creating new slide shows, and Chapter 6 for more detail on creating databases.)

With the exception of Outlook (Chapter 4), all Office 2003 modules let you:

- create new blank documents

- create new documents based on a "template"

- create new documents with the help of a "Wizard"

Sometimes, templates make use of Wizards, so it's often a case of mix-and-match.

Blank documents

Creating blank documents is the simplest route to new document creation; use this if you want to define the document components yourself from scratch. This is often not the most efficient or effective way to create new documents.

Templates

Templates are sample documents complete with the relevant formatting and/or text. By basing a new document on a template, you automatically have access to these.

Wizards

Wizards are advanced templates which incorporate a question-and-answer system. You work through a series of dialogs, answering the appropriate questions and making the relevant choices.

You also can create shared workspaces as a great way of working with other people on documents in real time. Workspaces are Windows SharePoint sites. You normally create a workspace when you send email with a document attachment.

In Outlook, hit Ctrl+N. Complete the email and insert a document (Insert, File). Hit the Attachment Options button – in the Task Pane, select Shared Attachments then enter the URL of a SharePoint site. From here, you need permission to create your workspace – see your site administrator for more information.

Documents created with the use of templates or Wizards can easily be amended subsequently.

Both templates and Wizards are high-powered yet easy to use shortcuts to document creation. Office 2003 provides a large number of templates and Wizards.

If this incarnation of the Task Pane isn't onscreen, click the down-pointing arrow and select New Document, New File, New Workbook or New Presentation, as appropriate.

If you're using Office Professional Edition 2003 (or the standalone version of Word 2003), you can create a new XML document and attach a schema (see page 209 for more information). Select XML document. In the XML Structure Task Pane, hit Templates and Add-Ins. Select a schema or hit Add Schema to locate one.

Re step 2 – in Access, you must also go on to create a new table. In the Access-specific dialog, select Create table by entering data then enter your own data. Alternatively, select Create table by using wizard and use the wizard.

(For how to do both, see Chapter 6).

1 In Word 2003, Excel 2003, PowerPoint 2003 or Access 2003, refer to the Task Pane on the right of the screen and do the following:

2 To immediately create a new blank document in Word, PowerPoint, Excel or Access, click Blank Document, Blank Presentation, Blank Workbook or Blank Database respectively

3 To use a dialog to create documents, click one of these options

4 If you selected On my computer in step 3, carry out the procedures on the facing page

5 Activate a tab

7 Preview templates and Wizards

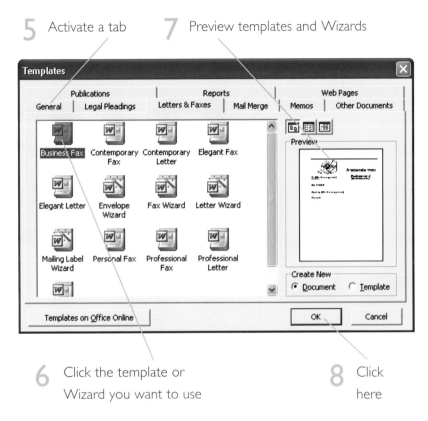

6 Click the template or
Wizard you want to use

8 Click here

9 Further dialogs may launch if you're using a template or Wizard –
complete these by following the on-screen instructions

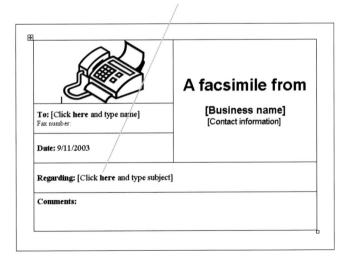

10 If you selected Templates on Office Online in step 3, use any of the templates on Office Online (for more on Office Online, see also pages 21–22)

If you base a new document on a template, Office creates a detailed document with preset (editable) text and formatting. If you use a Wizard, on the other hand, you get a succession of dialogs. Complete these as appropriate. The end result is the same as using a template: a feature-rich document you can edit as necessary.

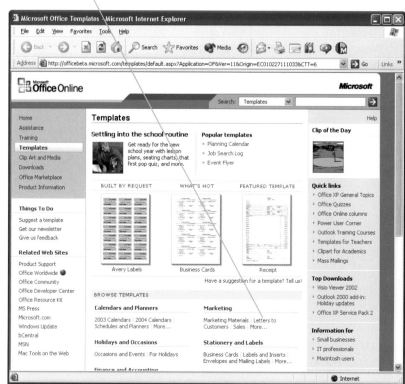

11 If you selected On my Web sites in step 3, use the dialog to search for templates on your networked websites

Opening Office 2003 documents

For how to open existing contacts or tasks in Outlook 2003, see pages 153 thru 154.

We saw earlier that Office 2003 lets you create new documents in various ways. You can also open Word 2003, Excel 2003, Access 2003 and PowerPoint 2003 documents you've already created.

In any module apart from Outlook, refer to the Task Pane on the right of the screen and perform steps 1–2 (if you haven't recently opened the relevant document, carry out steps 3–4 instead):

1 If your Task Pane is different, click the arrow and select Getting Started

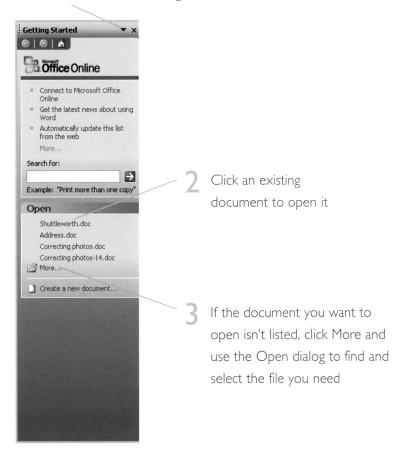

2 Click an existing document to open it

3 If the document you want to open isn't listed, click More and use the Open dialog to find and select the file you need

4 You can also launch the Open dialog directly from within any module except Outlook. Just press Ctrl+O

Opening Internet/Intranet files

You can view websites directly within Outlook –
see page 158.

From within any of the Office modules (apart from Outlook), you can open websites, Intranet sites or documents stored at FTP sites in your browser.

If the Web toolbar isn't currently on-screen, move the mouse pointer over any existing toolbar and right-click. In the menu which appears, click Web. Now do the following:

1   Ensure your Internet connection is live

2   Click Go

In Excel 2003, (providing you're using Internet Explorer 4.01 or higher) you can use these procedures to interact with Web-based spreadsheets.

For instance, you can enter data, create formulas, recalculate and sort/filter data and perform basic formatting, all directly from within the browser.

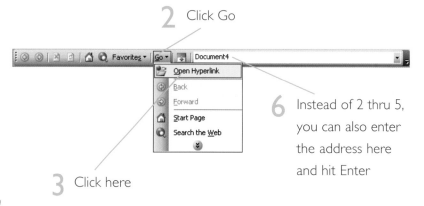

6   Instead of 2 thru 5, you can also enter the address here and hit Enter

3   Click here

4   Type in the relevant address

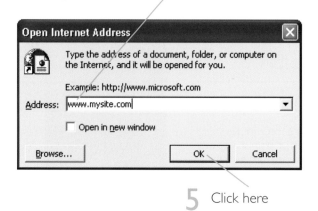

5   Click here

7   The Web/Intranet site selected in step 4 is opened in your browser

Saving Office 2003 documents

It's important to save your work at frequent intervals, in order to avoid data loss in the event of a hardware fault or power interruption. With the exception of Outlook, Office 2003 uses a consistent approach to saving.

Access 2003 saves data automatically.

Saving a document for the first time

In Word, Excel or PowerPoint, pull down the File menu and click Save. Or press Ctrl+S. Now do the following:

You can save your files in XML format. This is especially useful in Access but also applies to Word and Excel. XML is used to exchange data between dissimilar platforms and software. See pages 209 and 211 for more information.

In Word, select XML Document (*xml) in the Save as type field. In Excel, select XML Spreadsheet (*xml).

2 Click here then select a drive/folder combination in the drop-down list. Or click any buttons on the left for access to the relevant folders

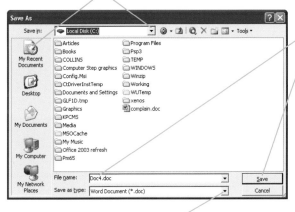

3 Type in a file name then click Save

Click here. In the list, click the format you want to save to

In Word 2003, you can use a special Wizard to create Web pages. In the New Document Task Pane, click On my computer... In the Templates dialog, select the Web Pages tab. Double-click Web Page Wizard and follow the on-screen instructions.

Saving previously saved documents

In Word, Excel or PowerPoint, choose File, Save. Or hit Ctrl+S

Speeding up saves

Choose Tools, Options. Select the Save tab then check Allow fast saves. When you're thru working with a document, uncheck this and save the completed file

Saving to the Internet

In any of the Office 2003 modules (apart from Access and Outlook), you can save documents (usually in HTML – HyperText Markup Language – format) to network, Web or FTP servers. You can do this so long as you've created a shortcut to the folder that contains them.

To create a shortcut to a Web/FTP folder, you must have a live Internet connection, rights to view/save files and its URL.

To create a shortcut to an Intranet folder, you must have a network connection, rights to view/save files and its network address.

Creating shortcuts to FTP folders

1 Open the Word, Excel or PowerPoint Open or Save As dialog:

2 Select Add/Modify FTP Locations

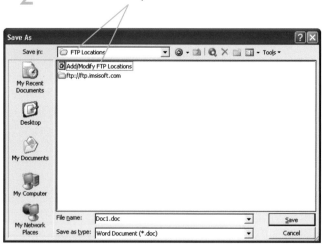

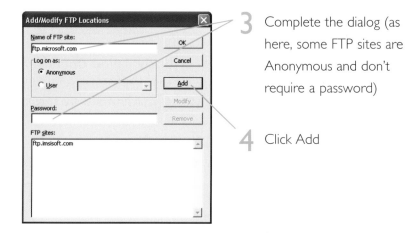

3 Complete the dialog (as here, some FTP sites are Anonymous and don't require a password)

4 Click Add

Creating shortcuts to Web folders

Creating shortcuts to local network folders may require a different procedure. See your system administrator.

Open the Word, Excel or PowerPoint Open or Save As dialog:

3 Click here

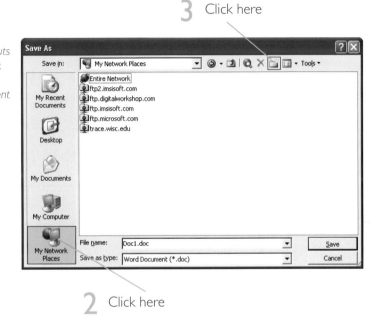

2 Click here

4 Complete the Add Network Place Wizard

Saving to Web/FTP shortcuts

Saving to the Internet in Access 2003 is more complex – see pages 209 thru 212 for more information.

Pull down the File menu and click Save As Web Page. In Word, click in the Save as type: field and select Web Page or Web Page, Filtered (the final option strips out most Word-specific formatting and produces much smaller file sizes); in Excel or PowerPoint, select Web Page

2 Complete the rest of the dialog in the normal way then select a destination shortcut and a destination format. Click OK

Saving configuration settings

You can use a special Wizard – the Save My Settings Wizard – to save configuration details in a special file (with the extension .ops). You can then restore the details contained in the file as a way of transferring your Office 2003 settings to another machine, or as a backup for your existing PC.

You could save configuration details on your website, as a handy backup.

Using the Save My Settings Wizard

1 Close all Office programs (not doing so can result in faulty configuration details being written)

2 Click Start, All Programs, Microsoft Office Tools, Microsoft Office 2003 Save My Settings Wizard then click Next in the first screen

3 Click Save... to save configuration details

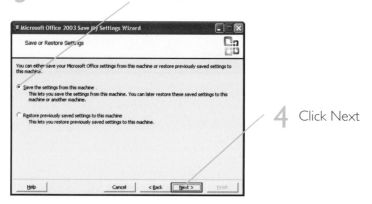

4 Click Next

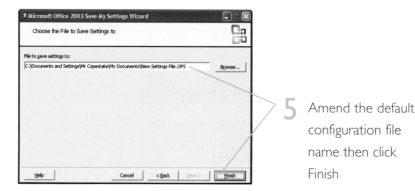

5 Amend the default configuration file name then click Finish

Using Office Online

Imagine a scenario. You're sitting at your desk, undertaking a typical Office task like working on an Excel spreadsheet, sending an email or designing a knockout Word document, when you hit a problem. What do you do (apart from not panicking)? The answer is, you use Office Online to find the answer you need.

Office Online is a special website which provides dedicated Office resources that are updated regularly in line with user feedback. There are links to Office Online in various of the Task Panes and menus you'll meet as you work thru this book. Office Online gives you helpful articles, templates, clips and training links.

Connecting to Office Online

1 The Getting Started Task Pane launches when you start any module apart from Outlook. If it doesn't, hit Ctrl+F1 then select it in the drop-down list

A lot of the help that Microsoft provides is only available on the Web, so it pays to use Office Online.

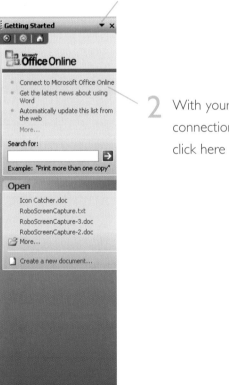

2 With your Internet connection live, click here

Office Online has several key areas. Use the following as guides (Office Online may have changed when you read this):

- *Assistance – hints and tips. Also module-specific help*

- *Training – links to tutorials*

- *Templates – lots of templates and some downloads*

- *Clip Art and Media – clips organized under headings*

- *Downloads – access to popular Office downloads and a link to Windows Update*

- *Office Marketplace – showcases non-Microsoft products and services*

- *Product Information – additional Office services*

3 Select an area then any link

4 Or search for what you want

5 If you carried out a search, click a link

Getting module-specific help

You can also search for help from within modules.

Type in your question in the Ask a Question box and press Enter

If you'd rather use Office Online directly to get help, you can hide the Ask a Question box to make more room onscreen. Choose Tools, Customize. Right-click the box and uncheck "Show Ask a Question box". Hit Close.

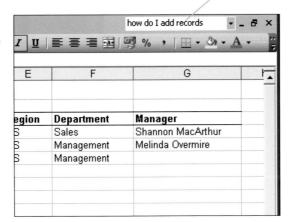

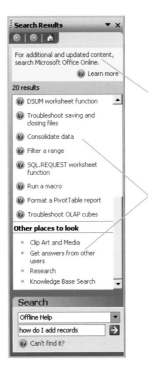

3 Or power up your Web connection and click here to launch Office Online

2 The Search Results Task Pane launches. Click any relevant entry (especially, click Knowledge Base Search to hunt thru the Microsoft Knowledge Base, a vast repository of problem-solving solutions)

Alternatively, use each module's HELP system.

Press F1

If your Internet connection is live, step 2 searches Office Online.

2 Type in search text (optimally, 2–7 words) then hit the arrow

3 Alternatively, fire up Office Online directly or select a specific link (Assistance, Training and Downloads are Office Online areas. Hit Communities for access to Office-specific forums)

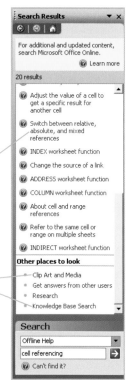

The Knowledge Base is a vast store of informational material and articles that Microsoft maintains for the benefit of users. You're almost certain to find what you need there.

4 After step 2, select a link in the Search Results pane

5 Or hit a suggestion. Try Knowledge Base Search if you need detailed help – Research refers to the Research Task Pane (see pages 78–80)

Quick File Switching

In order to use Quick File Switching you need to be using Windows 98 or later, or Windows 95 with Internet Explorer 4.0 (or a later version).

In the past, only programs (not individual windows within programs) displayed on the Windows Taskbar. With Office 2003, however, all open windows display as separate buttons.

In the following example, four new documents have been created in Word 2003. All four display as separate windows, although only one copy of Word 2003 is running:

Four Word 2003 windows

This is clarified by a glance at Word 2003's Window menu which (as before) shows all open Word windows:

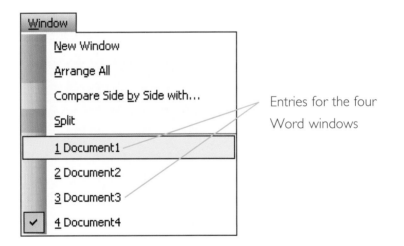

Entries for the four Word windows

1   To go to a document window, simply click its Taskbar button

2   Find Quick File Switching annoying? No problem. To disable it, choose Tools, Options. Select the View tab and uncheck Windows in Taskbar

Repairing errors

Office 2003 provides a special feature you can use to repair damage to modules.

Detect and Repair fixes Registry errors and missing files; it will not repair damaged documents. If the process doesn't work, reinstall Office 2003.

Detect and Repair

Do the following to correct program errors (but note selecting "Discard my customized settings and restore default settings" in step 2 will ensure that all default Office settings are restored, so any you've customized – including menu/toolbar positions and view settings – will be lost):

1 In any module, choose Help, Detect and Repair

2 Select one or both options

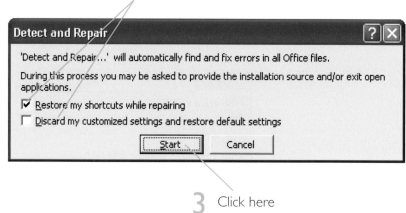

3 Click here

In Word and Excel, you can use another method to repair damaged files. Press Ctrl+O. In the open dialog, highlight the corrupt file and click the drop-down arrow on the Open button. In the menu, click Open and Repair.

(Word and Excel may run this procedure automatically when errors are detected.)

4 Follow the on-screen instructions – Detect and Repair can be a lengthy process

5 You may have to re-enter your user name and initials when you restart your Office applications

You can also use a further procedure for instances when an Office module "hangs" (ceases to respond).

Application Recovery

When errors occur, Word, Excel, Access and PowerPoint should give you the option of saving open files before the application closes.

1 Click Start, All Programs, Microsoft Office, Microsoft Office Tools, Microsoft Office Application Recovery

2 Select the program which isn't responding

Make sure AutoRecover is turned on to make it easier to recover documents. Choose Tools, Options. Select the Save tab and ensure "Save AutoRecover info every:" is checked. Customize the AutoRecover interval – the lower the better.

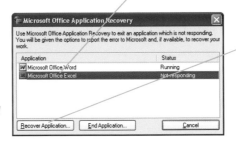

3 Click Recover Application to have Office try to recover the file(s) you were working on

4 Decide whether to email error details to Microsoft

Files with [Recovered] against them are usually more recent than those with [Original] in the title.

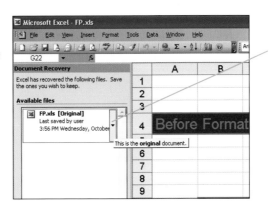

5 The module opens. Click the file you want to keep (usually the most recent) then select Open or View to view it or Save As to save it

This is the Document Recovery Task Pane – when you've finished with it, click the Close button.

Collect and Paste

You can copy multiple items to the Office Clipboard from within any Windows program which supports copy-and-paste, but you can only paste in the last one (except in Office modules).

Using Office 2003, if you want to copy-and-paste multiple items of text and/or pictures into a document, you can now copy as many as 24 items. These are stored in a special version of the Windows Clipboard called the Office Clipboard, which in turn is located in the Task Pane. The Office Clipboard displays a visual representation of the data.

Using the Office Clipboard

From within Word, Excel, PowerPoint, Access or Outlook, use standard procedures to copy multiple examples of text and/or pictures – after the first copy, the Clipboard should appear in the Task Pane. Do the following, in the same or another module:

To call up the Office Clipboard at any time, pull down the Edit menu and click Office Clipboard.

1 Click the data you want to insert – it appears at the insertion point

If the Clipboard Task Pane persistently refuses to appear after pasting, call it up manually and hit the Options button. Check Show Office Clipboard Automatically.

You must use the technique shown here to paste from the Office Clipboard: the normal paste commands like Ctrl+V only paste from the standard Windows Clipboard.

2 If you're inserting text, a Smart Tag appears (see pages 35–36)

3 To clear the contents of the Office 2003 Clipboard, click the Clear All button (or close all Office modules)

Word 2003

This chapter will get you up-and-running with Word in no time at all. You'll quickly get to grips with basic techniques such as entering, selecting and formatting text and using views. Then you'll move on rapidly and easily to advanced procedures that include the use of styles, proofing and summarizing text, inserting pictures, backgrounds and watermarks and customizing page layout/printing.

Covers

Chapter Two

The Word 2003 screen

Below is a detailed illustration of the Word 2003 screen:

Title bar   Menu bar   Toolbars

If the Task Pane isn't visible, hit Ctrl+F1.

The Status bar displays information relating to the active document (e.g. what page you're on).

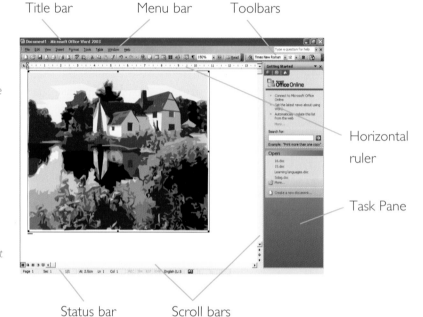

Horizontal ruler

Task Pane

Status bar   Scroll bars

You can protect your documents, so other users can only change the content or formatting in ways you specify. Choose Tools, Protect Document. In the Protect Document Task Pane, specify formatting or editing restrictions.

Some of these component – e.g. the rulers and scroll bars – are standard to just about all programs that run under Windows. Many of them can be hidden, if required.

Specifying which screen components display

Pull down the Tools menu and click Options. Then:

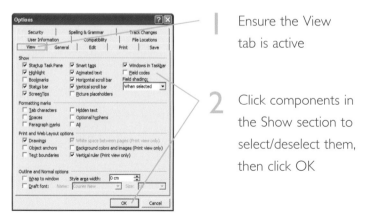

1 Ensure the View tab is active

2 Click components in the Show section to select/deselect them, then click OK

Entering text

You can also use Click and Type to enter text almost anywhere in a document, without inserting the necessary paragraph marks or formatting – see pages 33–34.

Word 2003 lets you enter text immediately after you've started it (you can do this because a new blank document is automatically created based on the default template). In Word, you enter text at the insertion point:

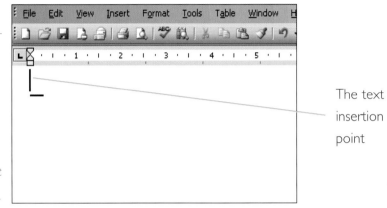

The text insertion point

You can have Word 2003 insert words or phrases for you – a handy timesaver.

Place the insertion point where you want the text inserted. Pull down the Insert menu and click AutoText. In the sub-menu, click a category then a glossary entry; Word inserts the entry.

Additional characters

Most of the text you need to enter can be typed in directly from the keyboard. However, it's sometimes necessary to enter special characters, e.g. bullets (for instance: ✍) or special symbols like ©.

Pull down the Insert menu and click Symbol. Do the following:

You can display AutoText entries on a toolbar. Right-click any toolbar and hit AutoText in the menu.

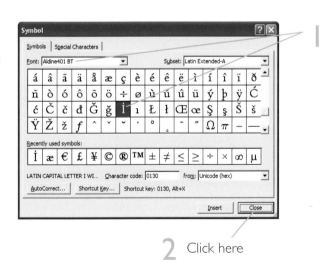

Select a font then double-click a symbol

2 Click here

Selecting text

Ctrl+A selects all text in the active document.

Word 2003 supports standard Windows text selection techniques. However, it also supports the following:

Selecting partial text blocks

| To select a rectangular part of 1 or more paragraphs, hold down Alt as you drag

You can also select text on the basis of formatting. Choose Format, Styles & Formatting. In your document, click in a word that has the formatting you want to select. In the Task Pane, click Select All.

"Office 2003 in easy steps" covers all the essential features of the latest version of Microsoft's leading office suite. If you want detailed, practical information with helpful, full-color illustrations – all organized in a concise, easy to understand format – this is the book for you!

"Office 2003 in easy steps" takes you through the suite's five modules: Word 2003 (word processor); Excel 2003 (spreadsheet); Outlook 2003 (personal/business information manager); PowerPoint 2003 (slide show creator); and Access 2003 (database). Its step by step approach ensures that you learn at your own pace. The first chapter emphasizes how the modules work together and shows you how to get started in any of them. Later chapters take each individual module and explain advanced techniques in a friendly, informative way, using plenty of walkthroughs. Finally, the book shows you how to use Office 2003's mail merge capability to create a letter, format it, insert the appropriate fields and then merge it with an Access database or your Outlook contacts to produce a highly tailored result which you can then print and/or edit.

Selecting multiple text blocks

Word has a special selection mode called Extended. Click where you want text selection to start. Double-click Ext on the Status bar. Now click anywhere in the document; Word selects all text between the two points. Press Esc to revert to normal selection.

| To select more than 1 text block, hold down Ctrl+Shift as you drag with the mouse

You can use a shortcut to select a paragraph. Position the mouse pointer on the left of the paragraph; it changes to an arrow. Now double-click.

"Office 2003 in easy steps" covers all the essential features of the latest version of Microsoft's leading office suite. If you want detailed, practical information with helpful, full-color illustrations – all organized in a concise, easy to understand format – this is the book for you!

"Office 2003 in easy steps" takes you through the suite's five modules: Word 2003 (word processor); Excel 2003 (spreadsheet); Outlook 2003 (personal/business information manager); PowerPoint 2003 (slide show creator); and Access 2003 (database). Its step by step approach ensures that you learn at your own pace. The first chapter emphasizes how the modules work together and shows you how to get started in any of them. Later chapters take each individual module and explain advanced techniques in a friendly, informative way, using plenty of walkthroughs. Finally, the book shows you how to use Office 2003's mail merge capability to create a letter, format it, insert the appropriate fields and then merge it with an Access database or your Outlook contacts to produce a highly tailored result which you can then print and/or edit.

Click and Type

You can create SharePoint workspaces in Word (see also page 11). Hit Ctrl+F1 then open the Shared Workspace Task Pane. Hit Create. If you encounter any problems from here on in, consult your site administrator.

You can also enter text in a special way in Word 2003, one that makes the process much easier. With Click and Type:

• you can enter text or pictures in most blank page areas, with the minimum of mouse activity

• you don't have to apply the necessary alignment formatting yourself – Word 2003 does this automatically (e.g. you can insert text to the right of an existing paragraph without having to insert manual tab stops)

Using Click and Type

In Web Layout, Reading Layout or Print Layout view, position the mouse pointer where you want to insert text or a picture. Click once – the pointer changes to indicate the formatting which Word 2003 will apply. The formatting depends on where you click.

There are some restrictions to the use of Click and Type. It won't work with multiple columns, bulleted or numbered lists or to the left or right of indents.

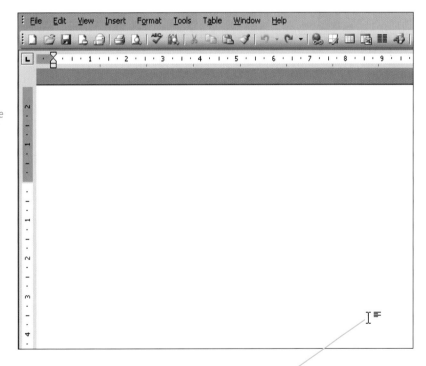

Here, the pointer shows that Word 2003 is about to left-align new text...

Now double-click, then do the following:

If you use Click and Type beneath an existing text paragraph, Word 2003 applies a specific style to the new text. You can specify the style used.

Pull down the Tools menu and click Options. In the Options dialog, activate the Edit tab. In the Click and type section, click in the Default paragraph style field. In the drop-down list, select a style. Finally, click OK.

If you find Click and Type confusing, turn it off. Launch the Options dialog/ Edit tab (see the tip above) and uncheck Enable click and type.

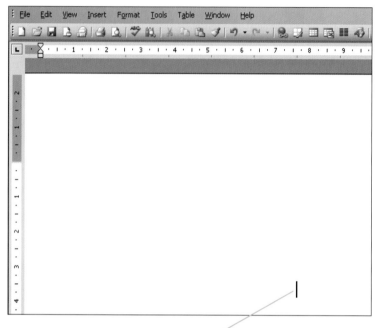

Begin entering text, or insert a picture in the normal way

The Click and Type pointers
The main pointers are:

Left-align

Center-align

Right-align

Left-indent

Using Smart Tags

Word 2003 recognizes certain types of data and underlines them with a dotted purple underline. When you move the mouse pointer over the line/box, an "action button" appears that provides access to commands which would otherwise have to be accessed from menus/toolbars or even other programs. Smart Tags are data-specific labels.

You can disable Smart Tags. In the Tools menu click AutoCorrect Options. In the dialog, select the Smart Tags tab and uncheck Label text with smart tags.

There are lots of different types of Smart Tag in Word 2003. For example, they can be names from your Outlook Contact list or from email recipients, dates/times, financial symbols or places.

Using Smart Tags

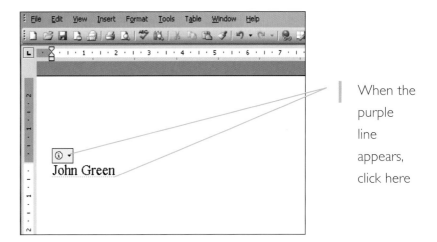

When the purple line appears, click here

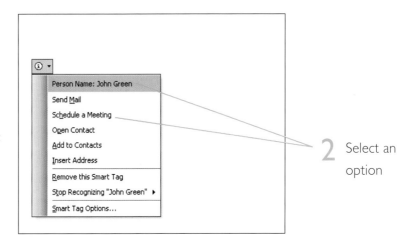

If you're into messaging with Microsoft Windows Messenger, Microsoft MSN Messenger or the Microsoft Exchange Instant Messaging Service, select Send Instant Message in the menu. Compose your message and then hit Send.

2 Select an option

Word also uses two additional action buttons that resemble Smart Tags in the way they work.

The Paste Options button

"Button" has been copied and the Paste command (Shift+Insert) issued...

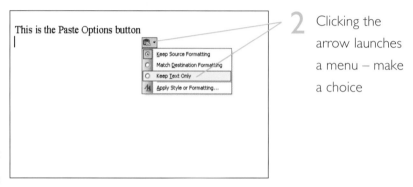

2 Clicking the arrow launches a menu – make a choice

Want more Smart Tags? Point your browser at http:// office.microsoft. com/marketplace /PortalProviderPreview.aspx? AssetID=EY010504821033.

The AutoCorrect button

An AutoCorrect entry has been set up which replaces "bu" with "button"

2 Clicking the arrow launches a menu – make a choice

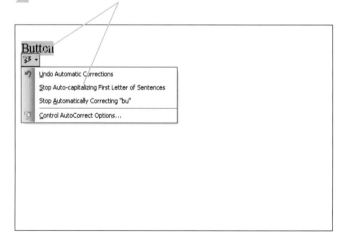

Sending email

You can use Word to write and send email messages (provided you've also installed Outlook as your email client).

To send email from Word, you must have specified Outlook 2003 as your Internet email program.

Within Internet Explorer, click Internet Options in the Tools menu. Click the Programs tab. In the E-mail field, select Microsoft Office Outlook. Click OK.

1 Open the New Document Task Pane then select E-mail message

2 Type in the recipient's email address

3 Type in a subject

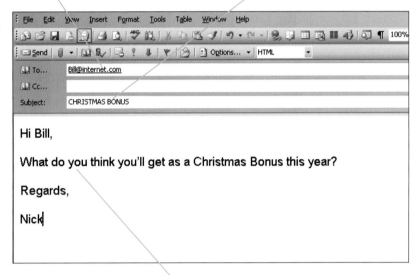

4 Type in your message

5 Click the Send button in the toolbar

Emailing a pre-written document

You may have to configure Outlook 2003's Remote Mail facility before you can send email. See Chapter 4.

1 Click this button in Word's Standard toolbar:

2 Follow steps 1, 2 and 4 above

Moving around in documents

To move to the location where you last made an amendment, press Shift+F5.
You can do this as many as three times in succession.

You can use the following to move through Word 2003 documents:

- keystrokes

- the vertical/horizontal scroll bars

- the Go To section of the Find and Replace dialog

The keystroke route

Word implements the standard Windows direction keys. Use the left, right, up and down cursor keys in the usual way. Additionally, Home, End, Page Up and Page Down work normally.

The scroll bar route

Use your mouse to perform any of the following actions:

The yellow box to the left of the vertical scroll bar is the Page Indicator. When you drag the box on the scroll bar in multi-page documents, the Page Indicator shows which page you're up to (but not in Web Layout or Reading Layout views.)

Click anywhere here to jump to another location in the document

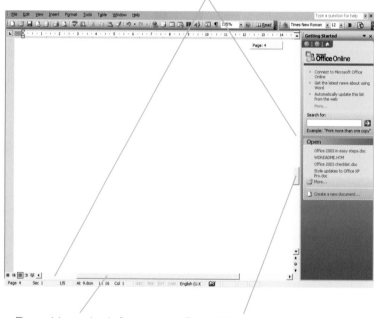

Drag this to the left or right to extend the viewing area

Drag this up or down to move through the active document

Footnotes and endnotes clarify or comment on text references. Footnotes appear at the bottom of the relevant page while endnotes print at the end of the document.

To insert footnotes and endnotes, choose Insert, Reference, Footnote. Choose Footnotes or Endnotes then allocate a number format and specify the number you want to count from.

The dialog route

You can use the Go To tab in the Find and Replace dialog to move to a variety of document locations. These include pages (probably the most common), lines, pictures, bookmarks and footnotes/endnotes.

Pull down the Edit menu and click Go To (or press the F5 key). Now do the following:

1 Click the location type you want to go to

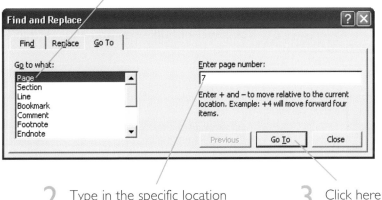

2 Type in the specific location reference (e.g. a number if you selected "Page" in step 1)

3 Click here

There are some useful refinements:

To have Word count the words in the active document, pull down the Tools menu and click Word Count. (Pre-select text to limit the count to this.)

- You can enter *relative* movements in step 2. For example, if you want to move seventeen pages back from the present location, type in –17. Or +5 to move five pages forward...

If you frequently need to word-count documents, you likely will find the Word Count toolbar useful. Right-click any toolbar and select Word Count.

- To move to the next or previous instance of the specified location (i.e. without specifying a reference), omit step 2. In step 3, the dialog is now slightly different; click Next or Previous, as appropriate. Click Close when you've finished

Views

Word 2003 lets you examine your work in various ways, according to the approach you need. It calls these "views". The principal views are:

Normal

Normal View – the default – is used for basic text editing. In Normal View, text formatting elements are still visible; for instance, colored, emboldened or italicized text displays faithfully. However, little attempt is made to show document structure or layout (for example, headers/footers, page boundaries and most pictures don't display).

For these reasons, Normal View is quick and easy to use. It's suitable for bulk text entry and editing.

To enter any view, pull down the View menu and make a selection. Or use the following keyboard shortcuts:

- *to switch to Normal view, hit Alt+Ctrl+N*
- *to switch to Print Layout view, hit Alt+Ctrl+P*

You can preview HTML files or documents (in your default Web browser) directly from within Word. Choose File, Web Page Preview.

In any view, Word now optimizes its display according to the current screen size and resolution, so text is even easier to read.

Normal View restricts what you view for the sake of quick text editing

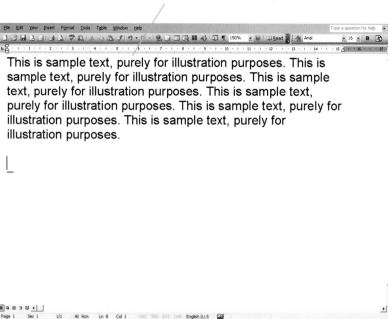

This is sample text, purely for illustration purposes. This is sample text, purely for illustration purposes. This is sample text, purely for illustration purposes. This is sample text, purely for illustration purposes. This is sample text, purely for illustration purposes. This is sample text, purely for illustration purposes.

Print Layout

Print Layout view works like Normal view, with one exception: the positioning of items on the page is reproduced accurately. Headers/footers and pictures are visible, and can be edited directly; margins display faithfully. In Print Layout view, the screen is updated more slowly. Use it when your document is nearing completion.

Too much "white space" (unused page areas) makes Print Layout unwieldy. Move the mouse pointer over the top or bottom of the page. Two arrows appear; click to toggle between hiding and displaying white space.

Print Layout uses ClearType technology – see overleaf.

Print Layout view displays everything

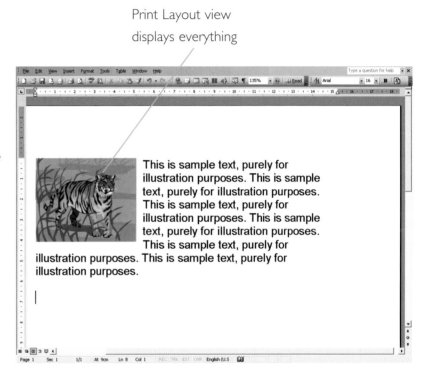

Web Layout

In Web Layout view, Web pages are optimized so that they appear as they will when published to the Web or an Intranet. Effects which are often used on the Web display (e.g. backgrounds and AutoShapes).

Reading Layout

Word 2003 offers a new concept: a view designed primarily for reading. It's also good for editing, too, though it may take you a little while to get used to it. Reading Layout view uses ClearType technology to make your reading experience even better – for more on ClearType, visit: **www.microsoft.com/typography/cleartype/default.htm.**

Reading Layout does not show how text will look when printed – for this, you need Print Layout view or Print Preview (Ctrl+F2).

1 To launch Reading Layout, hit Alt+R

Documents with wide graphics or text that isn't organized in paragraphs are best viewed in Print Layout.

2 To increase or decrease the text size, click one of these: ⊕ ⊖

3 To toggle between single- and multiple-page views, click: 🗐

ClearType may not be enabled by default in Windows XP (though Reading Layout view always uses it). To turn it on, activate Display in Control Panel. Select the Appearance tab. In the "Use the following method to smooth edges of screen fonts" box, select ClearType and hit OK. You should notice an immediate improvement if you're using a flat monitor or laptop.

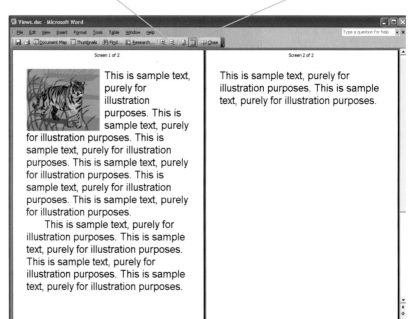

4 To view pages as they'll look when printed, click this toolbar button: 🗐

5 Esc takes you back to the view you were in before

Full Screen

Unless you have a particularly large monitor, you likely will find that there are times when your screen is too cluttered. Full Screen view hides all standard screen components in one operation, thereby making more space available for editing.

When Full Screen view is active, you lose access to toolbars and scroll bars. However, you should still be able to access the menus via the keyboard.

| | To enter Full Screen view (you can't from within Reading Layout), pull down the View menu and select Full Screen |

You can display documents side by side, for comparison purposes. With more than one document open, choose Window, Compare Side by Side with... Use the dedicated toolbar to refine this view. For example, hit this button:

This is sample text, purely for illustration purposes. This is sample text, purely for illustration purposes. This is sample text, purely for illustration purposes. This is sample text, purely for illustration purposes. This is sample text, purely for illustration purposes. This is sample text, purely for illustration purposes.

This is sample text, purely for illustration purposes. This is sample text, purely for illustration purposes. This is sample text, purely for illustration purposes. This is sample text, purely for illustration purposes. This is sample text, purely for illustration purposes. This is sample text, purely for illustration purposes.

to scroll both windows together.

Full Screen varies according to which view you were in when you launched it – this is Print Layout

| 2 | To leave Full Screen view, press Esc. Alternatively, click the Close Full Screen button |

Document Map

Use the Document Map as an aid to navigating through a document. Headings display in a special pane on the left.

1 To enter or leave Document Map, choose View, Document Map

2 Click a heading to go to that document section

Dragging the divider will resize the Document Map pane.

You don't have to resize the pane to make a partially hidden heading more readable; instead, just rest the mouse pointer over the heading.

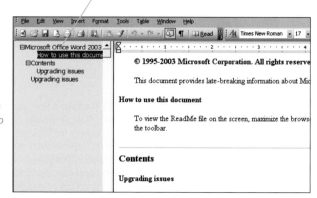

Thumbnails view

You can also have all document pages display as thumbnails.

1 To view or hides thumbnails (though not in Web Layout view or the Document Map), choose View, Thumbnails

2 Click a thumbnail to go to that page

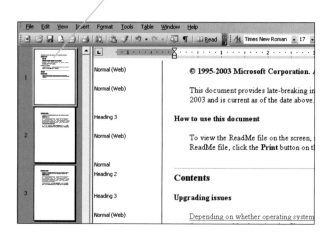

Summarizing documents

In effect, Word provides another way to view a document: you can "summarize" it. When you summarize a document, Word 2003 analyzes it and allocates a "score" to each sentence (sentences with repeated words get a higher one). After this, you specify what percentage of the higher-scoring sentences you want to display.

Documents need to be structured to respond well to summarizing. So use it primarily for reports and articles. (Emails generally aren't suitable.)

1 Pull down the Tools menu and click AutoSummarize – Word 2003 carries out the initial analysis

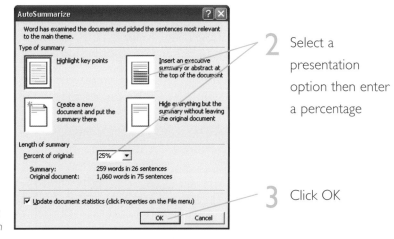

Summarizing other folks' work may infringe copyright laws.

2 Select a presentation option then enter a percentage

3 Click OK

AutoSummarize also works with a number of foreign languages (such as Italian, French and Spanish).

4 Here, Word has highlighted key points. Use the toolbar to fine-tune the appearance then review the summary

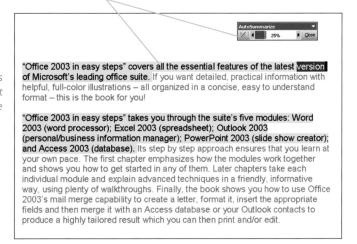

Regard the summarization as a rough draft that may require more work before it's ready to use.

Changing zoom levels

The ability to vary the level of magnification for the active document is often useful. Sometimes, it's helpful to "zoom out" (i.e. decrease the magnification) so that you can take an overview; at other times, you'll need to "zoom in" (increase it) to work in greater detail. You can:

You can't use Zoom in Reading Layout view. Instead, increase the text size.

- choose from preset zoom levels or specify your own

- choose Many Pages, to view a specific number of pages

Setting the zoom level

Pull down the View menu and click Zoom. Now carry out steps 1 or 2 (to specify a zoom %) OR 3 & 4 (to specify a group of pages). Finally, in either case, follow step 5.

The Zoom dialog varies a tad depending on the view you're using.

Folks with disabilities can find additional help in making Word accessible on the Microsoft Accessibility website on: www.microsoft.com /enable/default.aspx.

1 Click a preset zoom level

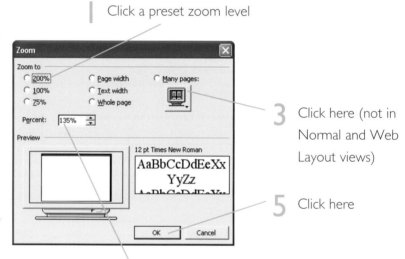

3 Click here (not in Normal and Web Layout views)

5 Click here

2 Type in your own zoom percentage (in the range 10%–500%)

4 Click a multiple-page view

Changing the font or type size

Word distinguishes between character and paragraph formatting. Character formatting alters the appearance of selected text while paragraph formatting affects the structure and layout of paragraphs of text.

Character formatting can be changed in two ways.

Applying a new font/type size – the dialog route

First, select the text whose typeface and/or type size you want to amend. Pull down the Format menu and click Font. Now carry out step 1. Perform step 2 and/or 3. Finally, carry out step 4:

1 Ensure the Font tab is active

It's sometimes helpful to kern characters (usually in headings) because they're too close or too far apart to be aesthetically pleasing.
  Select the Character Spacing tab. Check Kerning for fonts and specify the smallest typeface size you want Word to kern.

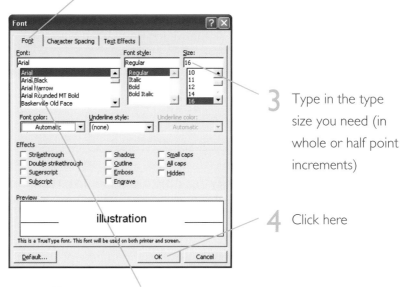

3 Type in the type size you need (in whole or half point increments)

4 Click here

2 Click the font you want to use

You can also kern pre-selected characters. Select the Character Spacing tab then Expanded or Condensed in the Spacing box. Specify an amount in the By box.

Applying a new font/type size – the toolbar route

Make sure the Formatting toolbar is visible. Now select the text you want to amend and do the following:

Click here; select the font you want to use in the drop-down list

Ctrl+] increases the type size by 1 point and Ctrl+[reduces it by the same amount.

Type in the type size you need and press Enter

Changing text color

First, select the text you want to alter. Pull down the Format menu and click Font. Now do the following:

Ensure the Font tab is active

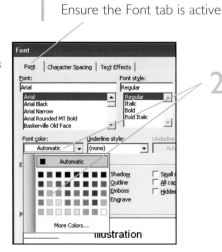

2 Click here, select a color then click OK (clicking Automatic sets the color to black, unless you've amended the default Windows text color)

Verifying current text formatting

If you're unsure about what formatting attributes are associated with text, press Shift+F1. Now click in the text. This is the result:

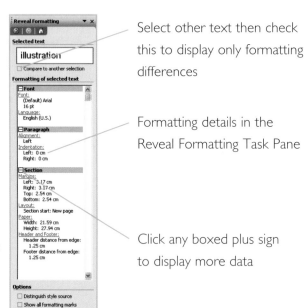

Select other text then check this to display only formatting differences

Formatting details in the Reveal Formatting Task Pane

Click any boxed plus sign to display more data

Font effects

You can also use the following handy keyboard shortcuts to apply effects:

Ctrl++	Superscript
Ctrl+=	Subscript
Ctrl+Shift+K	Small Caps
Ctrl+Shift+A	All Caps
Ctrl+Shift+H	Hidden

The following are the principal font effects:

- Strikethrough – e.g. ~~font effect~~

- Superscript – e.g. f$^{\text{ont effect}}$

- Subscript – e.g. f$_{\text{ont effect}}$

- All Caps – e.g. FONT EFFECT

- Small Caps – e.g. FONT EFFECT

In addition, you can mark text as hidden, which means that it doesn't display on screen or print.

Applying font effects

First, select the relevant text. Pull down the Format menu and click Font. Then carry out the following steps:

Ensure the Font tab is active

Many of the font effects can be combined – e.g. Superscript with Small Caps. However, Small Caps and All Caps are mutually exclusive.

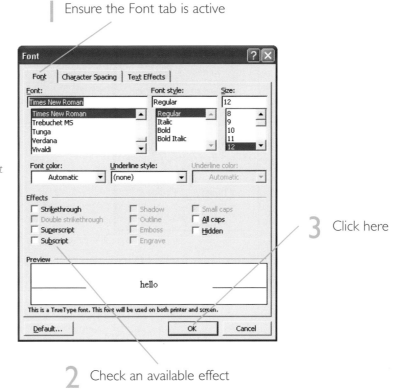

3 Click here

2 Check an available effect

Using the Format Gallery

A great way to apply consistent, coordinated formatting in a fraction of the time it would take otherwise is to use the Format Gallery. The formatting changes that the Format Gallery applies are directly related to Word's templates and so provide excellent results in just about any document that contains text.

Blanket formatting

When you apply formats to the whole of a document, they aren't applied by styles. Instead, Word searches for similar formatting and applies them on this basis.

1 Choose Format, Format Gallery

2 Select the Format All tab

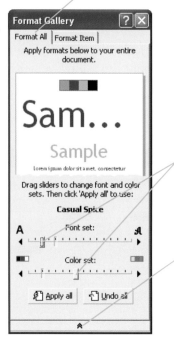

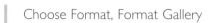

3 Drag the Font and Color set sliders to the formatting that best fits the look and tone you want for your document

You can also add formatting that you want to reuse in the future. Pre-select it then click the Add button on the Format Item tab.

4 Click the chevrons to "roll-up" the Format Gallery into just a menu bar – repeat to restore

Selective formatting

To apply formatting you've added to the Format Gallery, pre-select the text you want to format then select your formatting at the base of the Format Item tab.

1 Pre-select the text you want to format

2 In the Format Gallery, select the Format Item tab

3 Click the Font Set and/or Color Set buttons and select formatting from the list

Indenting text – an overview

Indents are a crucial component of document layout. For instance, in most document types, indenting the first line of paragraphs (i.e. moving it inwards away from the left page margin) makes the text much more legible.

Other document types – e.g. bibliographies – can use the following:

- negative indents (where the direction of indent is towards and beyond the left margin)

- hanging indents (where the first line is unaltered, while subsequent lines are indented)

- full indents (where the entire paragraph is indented away from the left and/or the right margins)

Some of the potential indent combinations are shown in the illustration below:

> This paragraph has a full left and right indent. It's best, however, not to overdo the extent of the indent: 0.35 inches is often more than adequate.
>
>   This paragraph has a first-line indent. This type of indent is suitable for most document types. It's best, however, not to overdo the extent of the indent: 0.35 inches is often more than adequate.
>
> This paragraph has a negative left indent. It's best, however, not to overdo the extent of the indent: 0.35 inches is often more than adequate.
>
> This paragraph has a hanging indent. It's best, however, not to overdo the extent of the indent: 0.35 inches is often more than adequate.

Left & right indent

First-line indent

Negative left indent

Hanging indent

Left and right margins (inserted for illustration purposes)

Applying indents to paragraphs

Indenting text – the dialog route

Select the paragraph(s) you want to indent. Pull down the Format menu and click Paragraph. Follow step 1 below. If you want a left or right indent, carry out step 2. To achieve a first-line or hanging indent, follow step 3. Finally, carry out step 4.

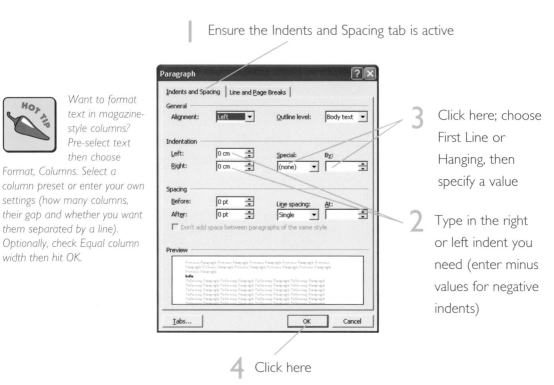

Ensure the Indents and Spacing tab is active

Want to format text in magazine-style columns? Pre-select text then choose Format, Columns. Select a column preset or enter your own settings (how many columns, their gap and whether you want them separated by a line). Optionally, check Equal column width then hit OK.

3 Click here; choose First Line or Hanging, then specify a value

2 Type in the right or left indent you need (enter minus values for negative indents)

4 Click here

Indenting text – the toolbar route

First, select the relevant paragraph(s). Ensure the Formatting toolbar is visible. Then click one of these:

Increases the indent

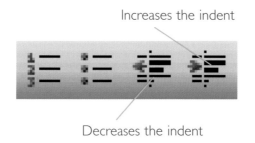

Decreases the indent

Indenting text – the ruler route

You can also use the horizontal ruler to set indents.

If the ruler isn't onscreen, pull down the View menu and hit Ruler

You can insert
indents when you
press the Tab key.
Select Tools,
AutoCorrect
Options. Click the AutoFormat As
You Type tab then check "Set
left- and first-indent with tabs
and backspaces". Now:

- to indent the first line of a
  paragraph, click in front of it
- to set a hanging indent, click
  in front of any line except the
  first

In either case, now hit Tab.

2 Drag to set a
first-line indent

3 Drag to set a
hanging indent

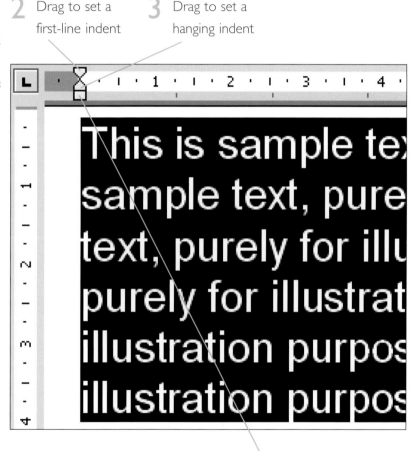

4 Drag to set a left indent

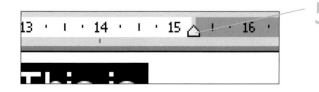

5 On the right
of the Ruler,
set the right
indent

Aligning paragraphs

Word 2003 supports the following types of horizontal alignment:

Align Left   Text is flush with the left page margin.

Align Right   Text is flush with the right page margin.

Justify   Text is flush with both the left *and* right page margins.

Center   Text is placed evenly between the left/ right page margins.

You can also align text vertically, relative to the top and bottom margins. This is a page-specific setting, so all the text on a given page is affected.

Pull down the File menu and click Page Setup. Select the Layout tab. In the Vertical alignment box, select Top, Center, Justified or Bottom.

Aligning text – the dialog route

First, select the paragraph(s) you want to align. Pull down the Format menu and click Paragraph. Now:

1 Select the Indents and Spacing tab

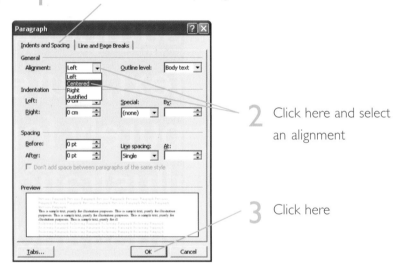

2 Click here and select an alignment

3 Click here

Aligning text – the toolbar route

Select the relevant paragraph(s). Then click one of these:

Align Left   Justify

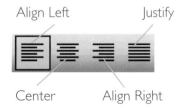

Center   Align Right

Paragraph spacing adjustments

Specifying paragraph spacing

Word 2003 lets you customize the vertical space before and/or after text paragraphs. This is a useful device for increasing text legibility.

By default, Word defines paragraph spacing – like type sizes – in point sizes. However, you can enter measurements in different units by applying any of the following suffixes to values you enter:

- in – for inches (e.g. "2 in")

- cm – for centimeters (e.g. "5 cm")

- pi – for picas (e.g. "14 pi")

- px – for pixels (e.g. "40 px" – about ½ inch)

You should find the following typographical/ computing definitions useful:

- *Picas are an alternative measure in typography: one pica is almost equivalent to one-sixth inch. Picas are often used to define line length*

- *Pixels (a contraction of "picture elements") are the smallest components of the picture on a computer monitor*

- *Points – approximately 72 points make one inch*

1 Select the relevant paragraph(s) then pull down the Format menu and click Paragraph

2 Ensure the Indents and Spacing tab is active

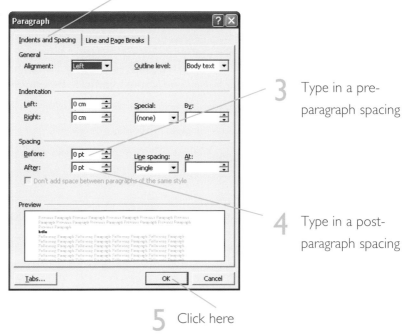

3 Type in a pre-paragraph spacing

4 Type in a post-paragraph spacing

5 Click here

This is sample text, purely for illustration purposes. This is sample text, purely for illustration purposes. This is sample text, purely for illustration purposes. This is sample text, purely for illustration purposes. This is sample text, purely for illustration purposes.

This is sample text, purely for illustration purposes. This is sample text, purely for illustration purposes. This is sample text, purely for illustration purposes. This is sample text, purely for illustration purposes. This is sample text, purely for illustration purposes.

This is sample text, purely for illustration purposes. This is sample text, purely for illustration purposes. This is sample text, purely for illustration purposes. This is sample text, purely for illustration purposes.

15pt before and after paragraph spacing has been applied to the red text

You can use these keyboard shortcuts to adjust line spacing:

Ctrl+1   *Single spacing*

Ctrl+5   *1 ½ spacing*

Ctrl+2   *Double spacing*

Specifying line spacing

Line spacing (also known as leading – pronounced "ledding") is the vertical distance between individual lines of text. The standard line spacing is single. However, some types of writing require a non-standard line spacing. You can apply the following types of leading:

Single
Each line of type is separated by an amount slightly greater than the type size. This is the default. Use Single for most writing types.

1.5 Lines
150% of single line spacing.

Double
200% of single line spacing.

At Least
Sets the minimum line height at the value you specify.

Exactly
Sets the value you specify as an unvarying line height: Word 2003 cannot adjust it.

Multiple
Sets line height as a multiple of single-spaced text. (For example, specifying "3.5" here initiates a line height of 3.5 lines.)

You can also use this technique to set the line spacing just before you begin to enter text.

1 Select the relevant paragraph(s) then pull down the Format menu and click Paragraph

2 Perform step 3 below. If you want to apply a preset spacing, follow step 4. To implement your own spacing, carry out steps 5 and 6 instead. Finally, follow step 7:

3 Ensure the Indents and Spacing tab is active

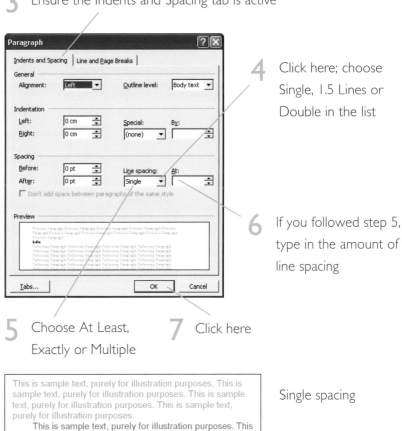

4 Click here; choose Single, 1.5 Lines or Double in the list

6 If you followed step 5, type in the amount of line spacing

5 Choose At Least, Exactly or Multiple

7 Click here

This is sample text, purely for illustration purposes. This is sample text, purely for illustration purposes. This is sample text, purely for illustration purposes. This is sample text, purely for illustration purposes.

    This is sample text, purely for illustration purposes. This is sample text, purely for illustration purposes. This is sample text, purely for illustration purposes. This is sample text, purely for illustration purposes.

    This is sample text, purely for illustration purposes. This is sample text, purely for illustration purposes. This is sample text, purely for illustration purposes.

Single spacing

1½ spacing

Double spacing

Paragraph borders

You can also border selected text within a paragraph. However, the Borders tab is then slightly different (e.g. you can't deselect the border for specific sides).

By default, Word 2003 does not border paragraph text. However, you can apply a wide selection of borders if you want. You can specify the type and thickness of the border, the number of sides, the color, whether the text is shadowed/3-D and the separating distance.

Applying a border

Select the paragraph(s) you want to border then pull down the Format menu and click Borders and Shading. Carry out step 1. Now carry out steps 2–5, as appropriate. Finally, perform step 6:

Want to border a whole page? Select the Page Border tab then complete the dialog using the steps on the right as a guide.

To set the distance from the border to the enclosed text, click Options. Insert the relevant distances and click OK. Then follow step 6.

Use step 5 to deselect the top, bottom, left or right paragraph borders. If you want to deselect more than one, repeat step 5 as often as necessary.

1 Ensure the Borders tab is active

4 Click a border option to border all four sides of the text

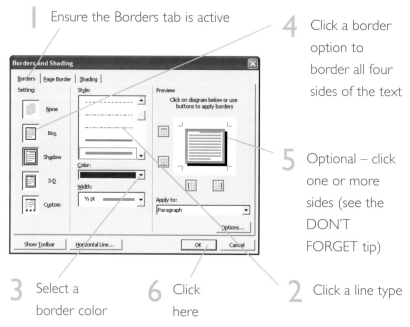

5 Optional – click one or more sides (see the DON'T FORGET tip)

3 Select a border color

6 Click here

2 Click a line type

This is sample text, purely for illustration purposes. This is sample text, purely for illustration purposes. This is sample text, purely for illustration purposes. This is sample text, purely for illustration purposes. This is sample text, purely for illustration purposes.

Experiment with border combinations

Paragraph fills

By default, Word 2003 does not apply a fill to text paragraphs. However, you can do the following if you want:

- specify a fill e.g. 20% (light gray) or 85% (dark gray)

- apply a simple pattern, if required

- specify a background fill or pattern color

Applying a fill

Select the paragraph(s) you want to fill then pull down the Format menu and click Borders and Shading. Now carry out step 1 below. Follow steps 2, 3 or 4 as appropriate. Finally, carry out step 5:

1 Ensure the Shading tab is active

4 Click a background fill color

Want to achieve unique blends? Experiment with applying different pattern and background colors.

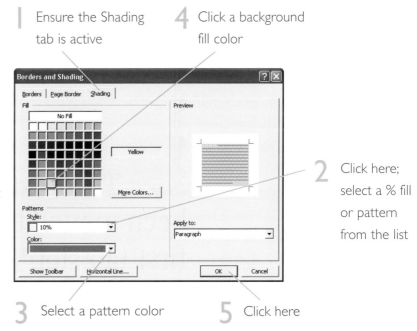

2 Click here; select a % fill or pattern from the list

3 Select a pattern color

5 Click here

This is sample text, purely for illustration purposes. This is sample text, purely for illustration purposes. This is sample text, purely for illustration purposes. This is sample text, purely for illustration purposes. This is sample text, purely for illustration purposes.

10%/Yellow

Working with tabs

Tabs are a means of indenting the first line of text paragraphs (you can also use indents for this purpose – see pages 51–53).

When you press the Tab key while the text-insertion point is at the start of a paragraph, the text in the first line jumps to the next tab stop – see the illustration below:

Never use the Space Bar to tab out paragraphs: this is because spaces vary in size according to the typeface and type size applying to specific paragraphs, and therefore give uneven results.

The first tab stop

The ruler (select View, Ruler to show or hide it)

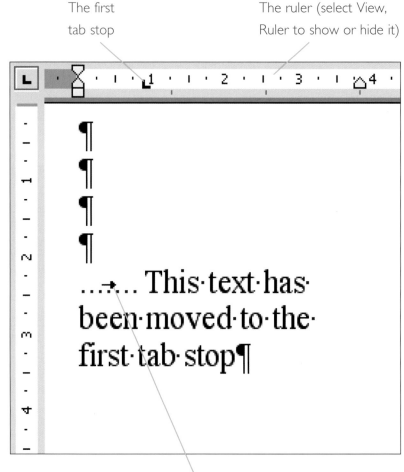

To have tab stops (and other symbols) display, pull down the Tools menu and click Options. Activate the View tab, then select All in the Formatting marks section. Finally, click OK.

Inserting tabs is a useful way to increase text legibility.

This arrow denotes the inserted tab (the dots are leaders – see the facing page)

By default, Word 2003 inserts tab stops automatically every half an inch. If you want, you can enter new or revised tab stop positions individually and with great precision.

Setting tab stops

1 Select the relevant paragraph(s)

2 Pull down the Format menu and click Tabs

3 Carry out step 4 below. If you want to implement a new default tab stop position, follow step 5. If, on the other hand, you need to set up individual tab stops, carry out steps 6 thru 7 as often as necessary. Finally, in either case, follow step 8:

5 Type in the new tab stop default

7 Click here

To change the unit tabs are measured in, pull down the Tools menu and select Options. Activate the General tab then click in the Measurement units field and select a new one. Click OK.

You can insert leader characters (a line that fills the space occupied by a tab). Just select an option in the Leader section of the dialog before step 8.

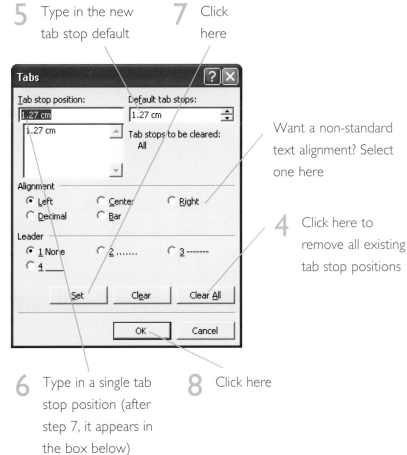

Want a non-standard text alignment? Select one here

4 Click here to remove all existing tab stop positions

6 Type in a single tab stop position (after step 7, it appears in the box below)

8 Click here

Searching for text

You can search for specific text within the active document. Even better, you can also search for character or paragraph formatting, either separately from the text search or at the same time.

For example, you can locate all instances of the word "information". Or you could have it find all italicized words, whatever they are. Similarly, you could have it flag all instances of "*information*" . . .

*You can widen your search with wildcards. For example, searching for "f?d" finds "fad" or "fed" but not "fatted" while looking for "b*n" locates "brain", "begin", "bitumen" and "bonus".*

For more on wildcards, press F1 over the Find dialog. Now click "Wildcards for items you want to find and replace".

You can also:

- limit the search to words which match the case of the text you specify (e.g. if you search for "Man", Word will not flag "man" or "MAN") – **select Match case in step 2 below**

- limit the search to whole words (e.g. if you search for "nation", Word will not flag "international") – **select Find whole words only in step 2**

To locate specific formatting, follow step 2. Then, in the extended dialog which launches, click Format. Word 2003 launches a menu; click the relevant entry. Complete the dialog which appears. Finally, start the search in the usual way.

- have Word search for word forms (e.g. if you look for "began", Word will also stop at "begin", "begun" and "beginning") – **select Find all word forms in step 2**

- have Word search for homophones (e.g. if you look for "there", Word will flag "their") – **select Sounds like in step 2**

Initiating a text search

Pull down the Edit menu and click Find. Now do the following:

Type in the text you want to find

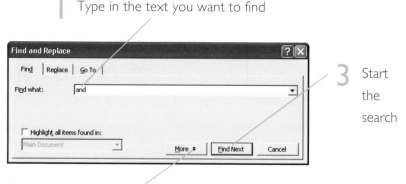

3 Start the search

To highlight all instances of the specified text, check Highlight all items found in. Select an area in the list then click Find All.

2 Optional – click More if the expanded form of the dialog isn't visible, then see the DON'T FORGET tip

Replacing text

When you've located text and/or formatting, you can have Word 2003 replace it automatically with the text and/or formatting of your choice.

You can customize find-and-replace operations with the same parameters as a simple Find operation. For example, you can have Word find every occurrence of "information" and replace it with "*information*", or even "*data*"…

Initiating a find-and-replace operation

First pull down the Edit menu and click Replace. In the Find and Replace dialog, click More. Now follow steps 1 and 2 below. Carry out steps 3 and/or 4, as appropriate. Finally, follow either step 5 OR 6:

1 Type in the text you want to find

2 Type in the replacement text

5 Click here to replace the first instance of the specified text

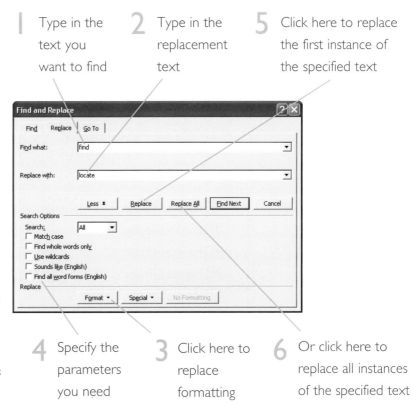

When you follow step 3, Word launches a menu; click the relevant entry. Then complete the dialog which appears in the normal way. Finally, carry out step 5 OR 6, as appropriate.

4 Specify the parameters you need

3 Click here to replace formatting

6 Or click here to replace all instances of the specified text

Searching for text in files

You can search for text within unopened files.

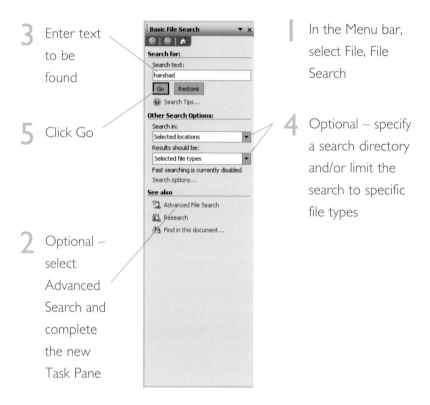

3 Enter text to be found

5 Click Go

2 Optional – select Advanced Search and complete the new Task Pane

1 In the Menu bar, select File, File Search

4 Optional – specify a search directory and/or limit the search to specific file types

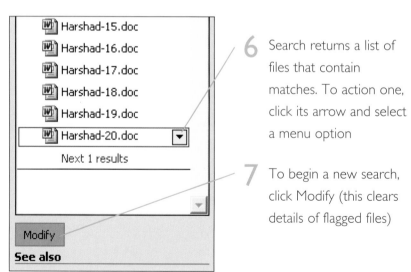

6 Search returns a list of files that contain matches. To action one, click its arrow and select a menu option

7 To begin a new search, click Modify (this clears details of flagged files)

Working with headers and footers

You can have Word 2003 print text at the top of each page within a document; this area is called the "header". In the same way, you can have text printed at the base of each page (the "footer"). Headers and footers are printed within the top and bottom page margins, respectively.

When you create a header or footer, Word automatically switches the active document to Print Layout view and displays the Header and Footer toolbar.

Inserting or amending a header

Working with footers is very similar. After step 1, click this toolbar button:

Word now shows the footer.

*You can also use this toolbar to insert the total number of pages (useful in this format: **page x of y**), add dates/ times, specify page setup options and hide document text (this makes it easier to work with headers and footers in complex documents).*

1 Move to the start of your document. Pull down the View menu and click Header and Footer

2 Insert (or amend) the relevant text

5 Click Close then format the text in the usual way

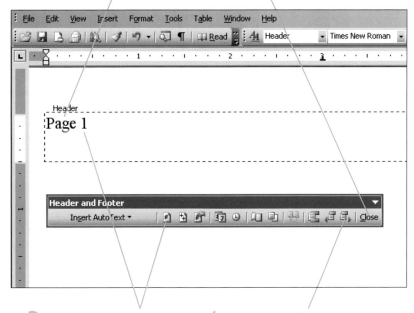

3 Click here to insert a page number

4 Optional – click here to move to the header on the next page

Inserting bookmarks

In computer terms, a bookmark is a marker inserted to enable you to find a given location in a document easily and quickly.

Creating a bookmark

Place the insertion point where you want the bookmark inserted (or select a text range). Pull down the Insert menu and click Bookmark. Now do the following:

Bookmark names must begin with a letter but can contain numerals.

To jump to a bookmark, select it in the dialog on the right then hit Go To.

Alternatively, hit Ctrl+G then, in the Go to what field in the Find and Replace dialog, select Bookmark. On the right, select a bookmark and hit Go To.

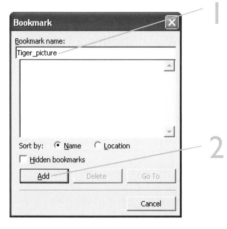

1 Name the new bookmark (you can only use one word – if you need more, use underscores to link multiple words)

2 Click here

3 By default, bookmarks are invisible. To view them, hit Tools, Options. In the Options dialog, select the View tab. Check Bookmarks. Bookmarks now display as brackets or I-beams

Be careful when you edit bookmarks. For example, if you cut and paste only part of the text within the brackets, the bookmark stays where it is. Also, any text you add between the brackets will be included in the bookmark.

This is sample text, purely for illustration purposes. This is sample text, purely for illustration purposes. This is sample text, purely for illustration purposes. This is sample text, purely for illustration purposes. This is sample text, purely for illustration purposes. This is sample text, purely for illustration purposes.

    This is sample text, purely for illustration purposes. This is sample text, purely for illustration purposes. This is sample text, purely for illustration purposes. This is sample text

Inserting hyperlinks

You can insert hyperlinks into Word documents. Hyperlinks are text or graphics linked to:

- another location (e.g. a pre-inserted bookmark) in the same document, or;

- a document on the World Wide Web or an Intranet

Creating a hyperlink to a bookmark

Select the text or graphic you want to be the source of the link. Pull down the Insert menu and do the following:

To amend a bookmark hyperlink, place the insertion point within it (for text hyperlinks) or select the picture (for picture hyperlinks). Follow steps 1–2. In steps 3–4, make the necessary changes. Finally, carry out step 5.

1 Hit Ctrl+K

2 Click here

4 Insert the text you want to display for the hyperlink

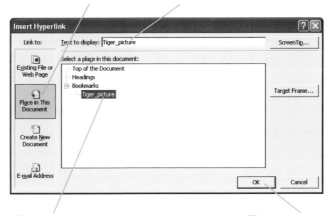

3 Select a bookmark or document location

5 Click OK

To delete a bookmark hyperlink, place the insertion point within it (for text hyperlinks) or select the picture (for picture hyperlinks). Follow steps 1–2. Now click Remove Link.

Bookmark hyperlink

Tiger_picture This is sample text, purely for illustration purposes. This is sample text, purely for illustration purposes. This is sample text, purely for illustration purposes. This is sample text, purely for illustration purposes. This is sample text, purely for illustration purposes. This is sample text, purely for

Creating a hyperlink to a Web/Intranet HTML file

To create a hyperlink to a document you haven't yet created, click Create New Document. In the dialog, enter the new document name/address, decide whether you want to edit it now or later and name the hyperlink. Finally, click OK.

1 Select the text or graphic you want to be the source of the link

2 Press Ctrl+K

3 Click here

5 (For text hyperlinks) insert the text you want to display for the hyperlink

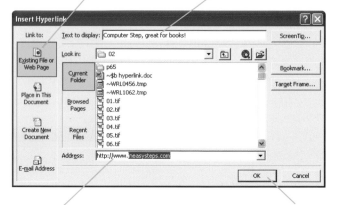

You can also create hyperlinks to any file: just use the Look in box to locate the file. It then appears in the Address box.

You can even link to specific locations within Excel or PowerPoint files. Just put # at the end of the file name in the Address box then enter:

- *the name of any named cell range within the Excel worksheet (for example: c:\new.xls#year_end)*

- *or the number of any slide within the PowerPoint presentation (for example: c:\newlaunch.ppt\#6)*

4 Type in the Web address

6 Click OK

7 A text Web hyperlink – Ctrl+click it to follow the link

Computer Step, great for books!, the best computer books in the store! Computer Step, the best computer books in the store! Computer Step, the best computer books in the store! Computer Step, the best computer books in the store! Computer Step, the best computer books in the store! Computer Step, the best computer books in the store! Computer Step, the best computer books in the store!

Computer Step, the best computer books in the store! Computer Step, the best computer books in the store! Computer Step, the best computer books in the store!

Creating a hyperlink to an email address

1 Select the text or graphic you want to be the source of the link

2 Press Ctrl+K

3 On the left of the Insert Hyperlink dialog, select E-mail Address

4 (For text hyperlinks) insert the text you want to display for the hyperlink

5 Enter the address and any subject you want the email to have

6 Click OK

7 An email hyperlink – Ctrl+click it to launch a new email in your email client with the address details pre-entered

You can enter email addresses on-the-fly in your documents – when you do this, Word automatically converts them into email hyperlinks.

This feature can become a mite intrusive at times. To disable it, choose Tools, AutoCorrect Options. Select the AutoFormat As You Type tab and uncheck "Internet and network paths with hyperlinks".

You can create hyperlinks via drag-and-drop, too. Right-click and drag text or a graphic from a Word, Excel or Access file into the file where you want the new hyperlink. In the menu, select Create Hyperlink Here.

Computer Step, the best computer books in the store! Computer Step, the best computer books in the store! Computer Step, the best computer books in the store! Computer Step, the best computer books in the store! Computer Step, the best computer books in the store! Computer Step, the best computer books in the store! Computer Step, the best computer books in the store!

Computer Step, the best computer books in the store! Computer Step, the best computer books in the store! Computer Step, the best computer books in the store!

Undo and redo

Word lets you reverse – "undo" – just about any editing operation. If, subsequently, you decide that you do want to proceed with an operation that you've reversed, you can "redo" it. You can also undo or redo a series of operations in one go.

You can undo and redo actions in the following ways:

Using the keyboard

You can undo most changes to images by clicking the Reset Picture button in the Picture toolbar.

1 Press Ctrl+Z to undo an action

2 Press Ctrl+Y to reinstate it

Using the Edit menu

1 Choose Edit, Undo...

2 Or choose Edit, Redo...

The dots denote the action being reversed or undone.

Using the Standard toolbar

1 Click here to undo the last action

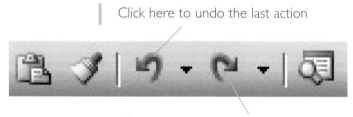

2 Or click here to redo the last action

3 To undo or redo multiple actions, click the arrow to the right of the Undo or Redo buttons

4 In the list, select 1 or more operations. If you select an early operation in the list (i.e. one near the bottom), all later operations are included

Inspecting text styles

Finding out which text style is in force

If you're in any doubt about which style is associated with text, you can arrange to view style names in a special pane to the left of text.

Pull down the Tools menu and click Options. Do the following:

1 Activate the View tab

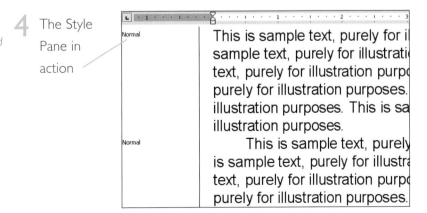

2 Type in a pane size (to hide the Style Pane, enter 0") then click OK

3 Pull down the View menu and click Normal (you can only view the Style pane in this view)

4 The Style Pane in action

Creating a text style

The easiest way to create a style is to:

A.   apply the appropriate formatting enhancements to specific text and then select it

B.   tell Word to save this formatting as a style

First, carry out A. above. Then pull down the Format menu and click Styles and Formatting. Now do the following:

You can also create new styles from scratch. Just hit New Style then use the New Style dialog to specify formatting for the new style.

Generally, new documents you create in Word 2003 are based on the NORMAL.DOT template and provide access to a variety of pre-defined styles, including some specialized ones aimed at the Web.

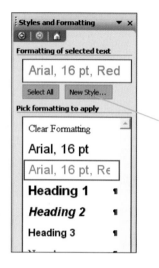

Click New Style

If you want any manual amendments you make to the new style to be automatically incorporated in the style (only in the active document, though), check Automatically update.

Check Add to template if you don't just want your new style to be available for the active document.

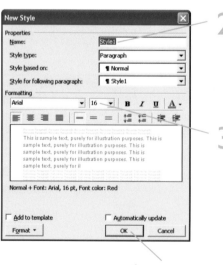

2 Name the style

3 Optional – adjust the style formatting (e.g. to increase or decrease the type size, enter a new one)

4 Click here

Applying a text style

Select the text you want to apply the style to

If you only want to apply the style to a single paragraph, place the insertion point inside it.

Pull down the Format menu and click Styles and Formatting

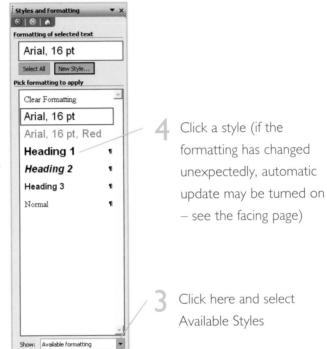

To delete a user-created style, right-click it. In the menu, select Delete. In the message, click Yes.

(When you delete a style, any text associated with it automatically has the Normal style applied to it.)

Click a style (if the formatting has changed unexpectedly, automatic update may be turned on – see the facing page)

Click here and select Available Styles

To remove formatting you've applied to text (in other words, to return it to the original style), select the relevant paragraph and hit Ctrl+Q. Or select characters and hit Ctrl+Spacebar.

Shortcut for applying styles

Word 2003 makes it even easier to apply styles – you can use the Formatting toolbar.

Select the text you want to apply the style to. Refer to the Formatting toolbar then do the following:

Click in the Style button; in the list, select a style (entries display with accurate formatting)

Amending text styles

The easiest way to modify an existing style is to:

A.   apply the appropriate formatting enhancements to specific text and then select it

B.   use the Styles and Formatting Task Pane to tell Word 2003 to assign the selected formatting to the associated style

First, carry out A. above. Choose Format, Styles and Formatting then do the following:

You can update paragraph styles automatically. Click the arrow to the right of a style in the Styles and Formatting pane then select Update to Match Selection. Now, changing the formatting of any text you've applied the style to will update the style.

Neat, but it's best not to use this feature for the default Normal style – this is because changes to Normal cascade down to lots of other styles like headers, footers and page numbers etc.

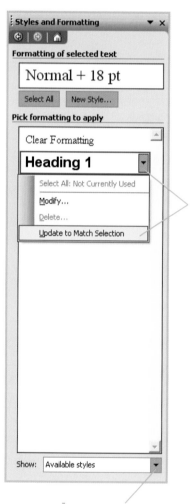

3   Want to specify that a specific style follow another? Right-click a style in the pane and hit Modify. Click in the "Style for following paragraph" box and select a style

2   Right-click the relevant style – in the menu, select Update to Match Selection

Click here – in the list, select Available Styles

Using the Styles Organizer

You can use the Styles Organizer to housekeep styles. You can also use it to copy styles between templates and documents.

1 Choose Tools, Templates and Add-Ins

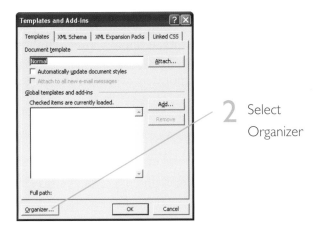

2 Select Organizer

To delete or rename a style, first select it in either window then select Delete or Rename.

3 Select the Styles tab

4 Select a style and hit Copy to copy it to the other window

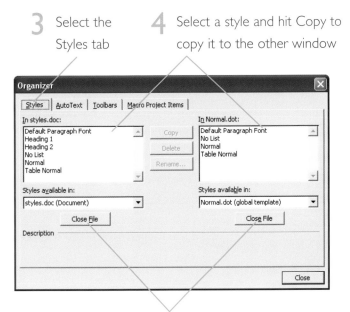

5 If the document/template entries shown in the fields flagged by step 5 aren't right, click the relevant Close File button. It changes to Open File; click this and select a new document or template

Spell- and grammar-checking

Word 2003 lets you check text in two ways:

*   on-the-fly, as you type in text

*   separately, after the text has been entered

Checking text on-the-fly

This is the default. When automatic checking is in force, Word 2003 flags words it doesn't agree with, using a red underline (in the case of misspellings) and a green line (for grammatical errors). If the word or phrase is wrong, right-click in it. Then carry out steps 1, 2 or 3:

1 Word often provides a list of alternatives. If one is correct, click it; the flagged word is replaced with the correct version

2 To have the flagged word or phrase stand, click Ignore Once

3 If the flagged word is wrong but can't be corrected now, click Spelling or Grammar and complete the resulting dialog (see the facing page)

Disabling on-the-fly checking

Pull down the Tools menu and click Options. Activate the Spelling & Grammar tab, then deselect Check spelling as you type and/or Check grammar as you type. Click OK.

Checking text separately

To check all the text within the active document in one go, pull down the Tools menu and click Spelling and Grammar. Word 2003 starts spell- and grammar-checking the document from the beginning. When it encounters a word or phrase it doesn't recognize, Word flags it and produces a special dialog (see below). Usually, it provides alternative suggestions; if one of these is correct, you can opt to have it replace the flagged word. You can do this singly (i.e. just this instance is replaced) or globally (where all future instances – within the current checking session – are replaced).

Alternatively, you can have Word ignore *this* instance of the flagged word, ignore *all* future instances of the word or add the word to its internal dictionary. After this, Word resumes checking.

Carry out step 1 below, then follow step 2. Alternatively, carry out step 3 or 4.

Grammar varies somewhat according to context. Word reflects this by offering two grammar styles: Grammar Only and Grammar & Style. Click Options in the dialog on the right then select a style from the Writing style box. (You can also customize each style. Hit Settings then specify which areas you want Word to check.)

If you're correcting a spelling error, you have two further options. Click Add to Dictionary to have the flagged word stored in Word's dictionary and recognized in future checking sessions. Or Click Change All to have Word substitute its suggestion for all future instances of the flagged word, as you type.

1 If one of the suggestions here is correct, click it, then follow step 2

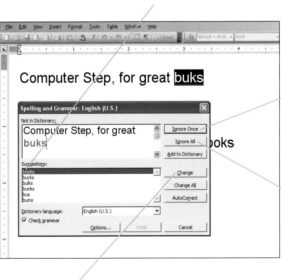

3 Click Ignore Once to ignore just this instance

4 Click Ignore All to ignore all future instances

2 Click Change to replace this instance

Searching for synonyms

Word lets you search for synonyms while you're editing the active document. You do this by calling up Word's resident Thesaurus. The Thesaurus categorizes words into meanings; each meaning is allocated various synonyms from which you can choose. The Thesaurus also supplies antonyms. For example, if you look up "good" in the Thesaurus, Word lists "poor" as an antonym.

Using the thesaurus

1 Select the word for which you require a synonym or antonym (or simply position the insertion point within it)

2 Hit Shift+F7

Antonyms have "(Antonym)" after their entries.

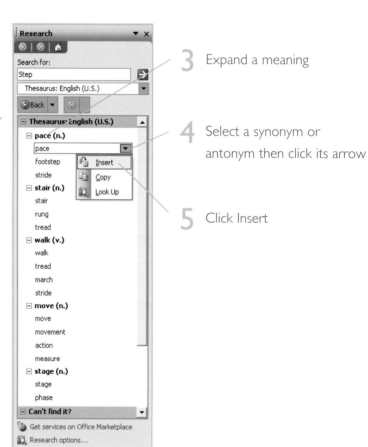

3 Expand a meaning

4 Select a synonym or antonym then click its arrow

5 Click Insert

Translating text

Word 2003 has a special Task Pane called Research. As we've just seen on the previous page, this incorporates a Thesaurus. However, it has a lot of other goodies as well, most or all of them online. Use the Research pane to find out all sorts of information. You can also use it to translate text into foreign languages.

Translating text

Be careful how much weight you attach to translation results. For example, "This cake is covered in nuts" translates in Italian as: "Questa torta è coperta in dadi". This is a bit hard to swallow since "dadi" means nuts (as in bolts).

You can also translate text within a document. Hold down Alt then click a word (or click pre-selected text to translate this).

1 With your Internet connection live, hold down Alt as you click once with the left or right mouse button

3 Enter the text you want translated

5 Click here

2 Select Translation

4 Select base and target languages

6 The translation appears here

7 Translation no good? Try some of the alternative options here

Research panel:
Search for: ripieno
Translation
Back

Translation
Translate a word or sentence.
From
Italian (Italy)
To
English (U.S.)
Translate whole document
Translation options...

Online Bilingual Dictionary
ripieno
1. *adjective* full; GASTRONOMY stuffed
2. *masculine* stuffing

Can't find it?
Try one of these alternatives or see Help for hints on refining your search.
Spelling alternatives
Search for any of the following:
ripen
repine
rapine
ripens
ripened

Get services on Office Marketplace
Research options...

Carrying out research

We've already seen how the Research pane can be used to translate text. You can do a lot more with it than this, though.

1 With your Internet connection live, hold down Alt as you click once with the left or right mouse button

3 Enter text you want to look up (as a general rule, try entering individual words or phrases and "building up" results)

Microsoft provides a course that you can take to familiarize yourself with Word's research facilities. Go to: **http://office.microsoft.com/ training/training.aspx?AssetID= RC010740391033&CTT= 1&Origin=EC010227221033& QueryID=MvA4BAErl** *(there are no spaces in this address).*

You can add your own favorite services (including intranet sites) to the Research pane. To do this, click Research options. In the Research Options dialog, check or uncheck services as appropriate. Or hit Add Services then type in the address for the new service(s) you want to add.

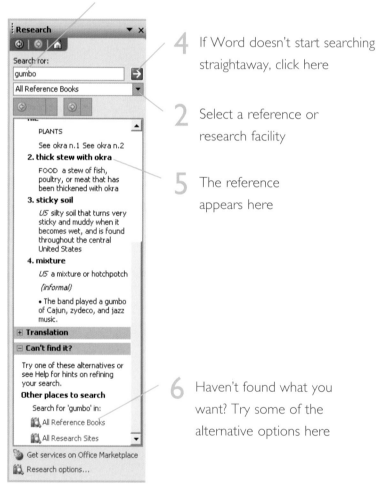

4 If Word doesn't start searching straightaway, click here

2 Select a reference or research facility

5 The reference appears here

6 Haven't found what you want? Try some of the alternative options here

Working with pictures

You can insert pictures automatically, by using Word's AutoCorrect feature.

To set up a picture as an AutoCorrect entry, select it. Pull down the Tools menu and click AutoCorrect. In the Replace field, insert the word/phrase you want the picture to replace. Select Formatted text. Click Add, followed by OK.

Word 2003 lets you add color and grayscale pictures to the active document. Pictures – also called graphics – include:

- drawings produced in other programs

- clip art

- photographs scanned in or imported from digital cameras (see page 84)

Pictures are stored in various third-party formats. These formats are organized into two basic types:

Bitmap images

Bitmaps consist of pixels (dots) arranged in such a way that they form a graphic image. Because of the very nature of bitmaps, the question of "resolution" – the sharpness of an image expressed in dpi (dots per inch) – is very important. Bitmaps look best if they're displayed at their correct resolution. Word 2003 can manipulate a wide variety of third-party bitmap graphics formats. These include: PCX, TIF, TGA and GIF.

To insert a picture stored as an AutoCorrect entry, type in the verbal trigger you set in the HOT TIP above. Now press Space or any other punctuation. Alternatively, press Enter.

Vector images

You can also insert vector graphics files into Word 2003 documents. Vector images consist of and are defined by algebraic equations. They're less complex than bitmaps and contain less detail. Vector files can also include bitmap information.

Irrespective of the format type, Word 2003 can incorporate pictures with the help of special "filters". These are special mini-programs whose job it is to translate third-party formats into a form which Word can use.

Compression

You can have Word compress images within documents (making them smaller).

1 In the Picture toolbar, click this button:

2 Complete the Compress Pictures dialog

Brief notes on picture formats

Graphics formats Word 2003 will accept include the following (the column on the left shows the relevant file suffix):

BMP   Windows Bitmap. A popular bitmap format.

CGM   Computer Graphics Metafile. A vector format frequently used in the past, especially as a medium for clip-art transmission. Less often used nowadays.

EPS   Encapsulated PostScript. Perhaps the most widely used PostScript format. PostScript combines vector *and* bitmap data very successfully. Incorporates a low-resolution bitmap "header" for preview purposes.

GIF   Graphics Interchange Format. Developed for the online transmission of graphics data over the Internet. Just about any Windows program – and a lot more besides – will read GIF. Disadvantage: it can't handle more than 256 colors. Compression is supported.

PCD   (Kodak) PhotoCD. Used primarily to store photographs on CD.

PCX   An old stand-by. Originated with PC Paintbrush, a paint program. Used for years to transfer graphics data between Windows applications.

TGA   Targa. A high-end format, and also a bridge with so-called low-end computers (e.g. Amiga and Atari). Often used in PC and Mac paint and ray-tracing programs because of its high-resolution color fidelity.

TIFF   Tagged Image File Format. Suffix: TIF. If anything, even more widely used than PCX, across a whole range of platforms and applications.

WMF   Windows Metafile. A frequently used vector format. Can be used for information exchange between just about all Windows programs.

Inserting pictures

Inserting pictures via the Clip Art Task Pane

You can use Click and Type to insert pictures in blank page areas.

1 Position the insertion point at the location within the active document where you want to insert the picture

2 Select Insert, Picture, Clip Art

3 Enter one or more keywords (these help you find clips)

5 Click Go

4 Optional – click here and make the appropriate choices

To add new clips to collections (or add new keywords to existing clips), click the Clip art on Office Online link at the base of the pane.

6 Click an icon to insert the clip

7 Want more clips? Click Clip art on Office Online for access to a wide variety (and a lot more besides)

Inserting pictures – the dialog route

1 Position the insertion point at the location within the active
document where you want to insert the picture

2 Select Insert, Picture, From File

4 Click here. In the drop-down list, click the
drive/folder that hosts the picture

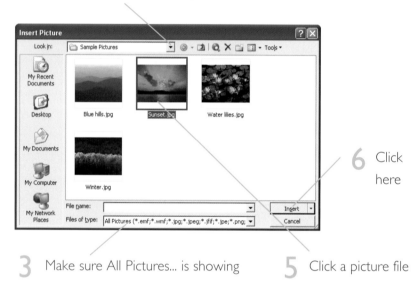

6 Click
here

3 Make sure All Pictures... is showing   5 Click a picture file

Inserting pictures via scanners or cameras

*Want to
customize the
acquisition? Click
Custom Insert
instead then
complete your device's dialog.*

1 Select Insert, Picture, From Scanner or Camera

*You can only
import from
TWAIN-compliant
devices.*

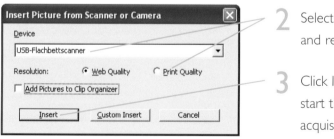

2 Select a device
and resolution

3 Click Insert to
start the
acquisition

Editing pictures

Once you've inserted pictures into a Word 2003 document, you can amend them in a variety of ways. First, you have to select the relevant picture. To do this, simply left-click once on an image. Word surrounds it with eight handles. The illustration below demonstrates these:

Handles   Rotate handle – drag to rotate

Only what Word calls "drawing objects" can be rotated – in other words, imported bitmaps such as photographs can't (do this instead in your photo-editing software).

Images that have the "In line with text" text wrap option selected also lack rotation handles; to correct this, impose a different wrap option (page 87).

If your image is not a bitmap and you still can't rotate it, try this. Select the image, then make sure the Drawing toolbar (View, Toolbars, Drawing) is onscreen. Click on the Draw button and select Ungroup. Repeat but on this occasion select Group.

1 To move a picture, just drag it to a new location

2 To rescale it, drag a corner handle to rescale proportionately, or a side handle to warp the image. Drag outwards to increase the size or inwards to reduce it

Using the Picture toolbar

When you import pictures or clip art, the Picture toolbar (View, Toolbars, Picture) should automatically launch. You can use this to make working with images even easier.

Complete any menu that launches after any of these steps (except for step 3 – you can use the dialog this produces to implement these and other changes).

1 Adjust the color

2 Adjust the brightness and contrast

3 Launch the Format... dialog

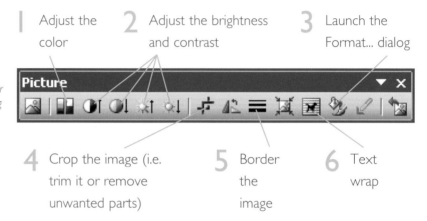

4 Crop the image (i.e. trim it or remove unwanted parts)

5 Border the image

6 Text wrap

Use this technique to apply basic borders. If you want more control, click More Lines at the base of the menu and use the dialog that launches to customize the effect you want.

The image from page 85:

- converted to black and white (step 1)
- brightness and contrast increased (step 2)
- cropped (step 4)
- bordered (step 5)

Text wrap

You can control how text wraps around a picture.

Alternatively, you can follow step 6 on page 86 then choose a wrap method from the drop-down menu.

To specify which sides wrap and the distance separating the graphic and text, hit Advanced. Complete the Advanced Layout dialog.

1 Double-click the picture

2 Select this tab

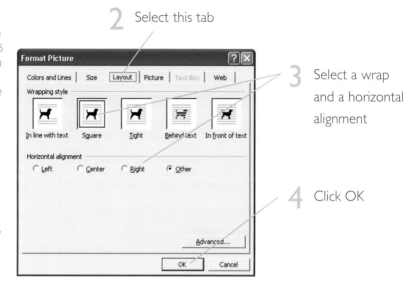

3 Select a wrap and a horizontal alignment

4 Click OK

"Office 2003 in easy steps" covers all the essential features of the latest version of Microsoft's leading office suite. If you want detailed, practical information with helpful, full-color illustrations – all organized in a concise, easy to understand format – this is the book for you!

"Office 2003 in easy steps" takes you through the suite's five modules: Word 2003 (word processor); Excel 2003 (spreadsheet); Outlook 2003 (personal/business information manager); PowerPoint 2003 (slide show creator); and Access 2003 (database). Its step by step approach ensures that you learn at your own pace. The first chapter emphasizes how the modules work together and shows you how to get started in any of them. Later chapters take each individual module and explain advanced techniques in a friendly, informative way, using plenty of walkthroughs. Finally, the book shows you how to use Office 2003's mail merge capability to create a letter, format it, insert the appropriate fields and then merge it with an Access database or your Outlook contacts to produce a highly tailored result which you can then print and/or edit.

5 "Square" wrap with Center alignment

Inserting WordArt

Word has a special feature called WordArt that lets you insert text with spectacular effects.

1   Position the insertion point at the location within the active document where you want to insert the decorative text

2   Select Insert, Picture, WordArt

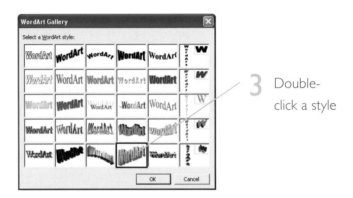

3   Double-click a style

4   Type in your text, select a font/type size/ text style and hit OK

Want to refine the WordArt text? Right-click it and select Format WordArt. Use the Format WordArt dialog to apply a different color or shape, wrap the text or resize it.

Inserting watermarks

You can add watermarks (graphics or text printed above or below document text) to Word pages but they only display in Print Layout view and Print Preview.

Adding a watermark

1 Pull down the Format menu and click Background, Printed Watermark

2 To insert a picture watermark, check Picture watermark then click Select Picture. Use the dialog to find/select a picture. Also, select a scale and – optionally – Washout (makes it much fainter)

Use this dialog to amend any existing watermark. To delete it, select No watermark.

If you change a document's header or footer after applying a watermark, it may not appear on every page. Reinsert the watermark.

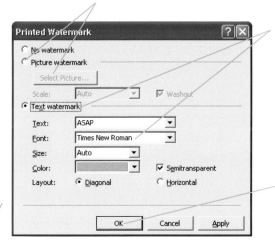

3 Alternatively, to insert a text watermark, select Text watermark and complete the text fields

4 Click here

This is sample text, purely for illustration purposes. This is sample text, purely for illustration purposes. This is sample text, purely for illustration purposes. This is sample text, purely for illustration purposes. This is sample text, purely for illustration purposes.

This is sample text, purely for illustration purposes. This is sample text, purely for illustration purposes. This is sample text, purely for illustration purposes. This is sample text, purely for illustration purposes.

This is sample text, purely for illustration purposes. This is sample text, purely for illustration purposes. This is sample text, purely for illustration purposes. This is sample text, purely for illustration purposes.

A picture watermark (without Washout)

Inserting backgrounds

Why not add pattern, texture or gradient backgrounds to Web pages? These are designed to enhance Web viewing but don't print. Backgrounds display in most views except for Normal.

Adding a website background

1 Pull down the Format menu and click Background, Fill Effects

2 Select a tab then complete the dialog. For example, to add a gradient fill, select the Gradient tab then either create your own effect or hit Preset and use a pre-prepared one

3 Click OK then choose File, Save as Web Page (see pages 18 thru 20)

Adding a gradient background to a website can make it much more effective

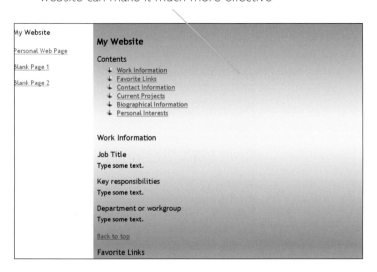

Page setup – an overview

You can control page layout to a great extent in Word 2003. You can specify:

- the top, bottom, left and/or right page margins

- the distance between the top page edge and the top edge of the header

- the distance between the bottom page edge and bottom edge of the footer

The illustration below shows these page components:

By default, page setup changes apply to the whole document. If you only want them to affect specific text, preselect it then choose Selected text in the Apply to box in the Page Setup dialog.

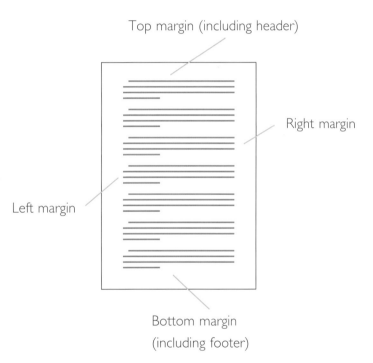

You can also specify:

- the page size (irrespective of margins and headers/footers)

- the page orientation ("landscape" or "portrait")

If none of the supplied page sizes is suitable, you can customize your own.

Specifying margins

All documents have margins, because printing on the whole of a sheet is both unsightly and – in the case of many printers, since the mechanism has to grip the page – impossible. Documents need a certain amount of "white space" (the unprinted portion of the page) to balance the areas which contain text and graphics. Without this, they can't be visually effective. As a result, it's important to set margins correctly.

Margins are the framework on which indents and tabs are based.

Customizing margins

1 Pull down the File menu and click Page Setup

Some documents (such as books and magazines) use "facing pages" layout, where the left and right inside margins are the same width. The outer margins are also the same. Click in the Multiple pages box and select Mirror margins.

2 Select the Margins tab

3 Type in the margin settings you need

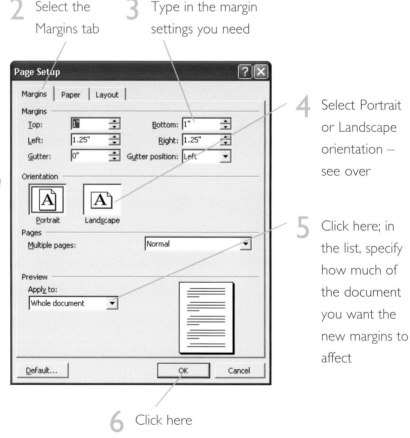

4 Select Portrait or Landscape orientation – see over

If you plan to bind your document, you'll need to set a gutter margin that increases the standard top or side margin. Select Normal in Multiple pages then complete the Gutter and Gutter position boxes.

5 Click here; in the list, specify how much of the document you want the new margins to affect

6 Click here

Changed the standard margin settings? Hit Default to implement your settings as a new default.

Specifying the page size

Whatever the page size, you can have both portrait and landscape pages in the same document.

Word 2003 comes with some 17 preset page sizes – for instance, Letter, Legal and A5. These are suitable for most purposes. However, you can also set up your own page definition.

There are two aspects to every page size: a vertical measurement, and a horizontal measurement. These can be varied according to orientation. There are two possible orientations:

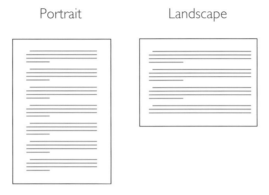

Portrait   Landscape

Setting the page size

1 Pull down the File menu and click Page Setup

Re step 3 – to create your own page size, click Custom size. Then type in the correct measurements in the Width and Height fields.

2 Ensure the Paper tab is active

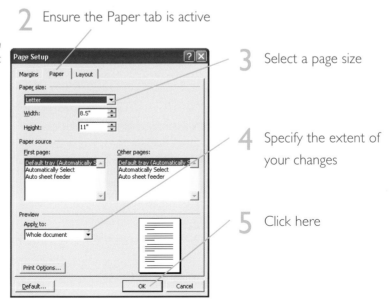

3 Select a page size

4 Specify the extent of your changes

5 Click here

Using Print Preview

You can use a special view mode called Print Preview. This displays the active document exactly as it will look when printed. Use Print Preview as a final check just before printing.

1   To launch or leave Print Preview, hit Ctrl+F2

Print Preview toolbar

You can hide all screen components apart from the Print Preview and the Full Screen toolbars. Click this button in the Print Preview toolbar:

To leave Full Screen view, press Esc.

2   To zoom in or out, ensure the cursor is a magnifying glass – if it isn't, click this button in the Print Preview toolbar:

Now position the cursor over the part of the document you want to expand and left-click once

3   To edit text directly from within Print Preview, zoom in on the text then click the button described in step 2. Now click in the text and make the necessary changes

4   To view multiple pages at the same time, click this button:

In the list, drag until you reach the correct view.

Printer setup

Most Word 2003 documents need to be printed eventually. Before you can begin printing, however, you need to ensure that:

The question of which printer you select affects how the document displays in Print Preview mode.

- the correct printer is selected (if you have more than one installed)

- the correct printer settings are in force

Word 2003 calls these collectively the "printer setup".

Irrespective of the printer selected, the settings vary in accordance with the job in hand. For example, most printer drivers (the software which "drives" the printer) allow you to specify whether or not you want pictures printed. Additionally, they often allow you to specify the resolution or print quality of the output…

Selecting the printer and/or settings

At any time before you're ready to print a document, pull down the File menu and click Print. Now do the following:

Click here; select the printer you want from the list

This procedure can also be followed from within Print Preview mode.

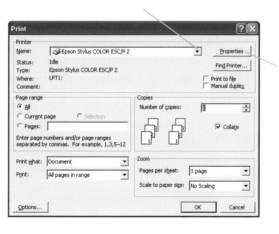

2 Click here to adjust printer settings (see your printer's manual for how to do this)

3 Complete the remainder of the Print dialog, prior to printing out your document

Printing – an overview

Mix and match

Once the active document is how you want it (and you've customized the printer setup appropriately), you likely will need to print it out. You can set a variety of options before you do so. These include:

- the number of copies you want printed

- whether you want the copies "collated" (the process whereby Word 2003 prints one full copy at a time). For instance, if you're printing three copies of a 40-page document, Word prints pages 1–40 of the first document, followed by pages 1–40 of the second and pages 1–40 of the third

- which pages (or page ranges) you want printed

- whether you want to limit the print run to odd or even pages

- whether you want the print run restricted to text you selected before you started

- whether you want the pages printed in reverse order

- the quality of the eventual output

- whether you want to go on working in Word 2003 while the document prints (the default). Word 2003 calls this "background printing". Disable this option if your system is short of memory

- which document components you want to print (for example, you can restrict the printout to document properties or styles)

Fast track

Alternatively, you can simply opt to print your document with the default options in force (Word 2003 provides a "fast track" approach to this). This is a much quicker process.

1   In any view, click this toolbar icon:

2   Printing begins immediately

Customized printing

If you need to set revised print options before printing, do the following:

Pull down the File menu and click Print. Now carry out steps 1–4, as appropriate. Finally, carry out step 5.

1 Uncheck this to deselect collation

2 Type in the number of copies

Some printing options can also be set via another route. Choose Tools, Options and select the Print tab.

To print only odd or even pages, click in the Print field and select Odd Pages or Even Pages.

To print more than one page on a sheet, click Pages per sheet. Select a number in the list.

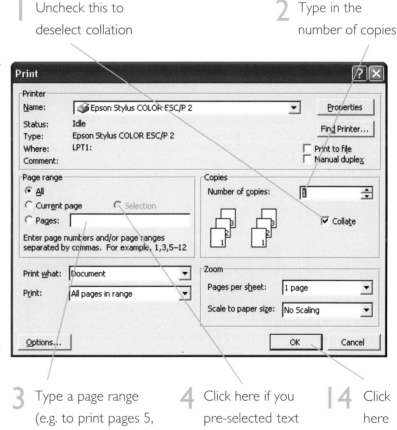

3 Type a page range (e.g. to print pages 5, 12 and 16 thru 20 type in "5,12,16-20". Omit the quotes)

4 Click here if you pre-selected text and this is all you want to print

4 Click here

5 To specify what part of the document prints, click in the Print what field and make a choice

6 For more options, carry out the actions overleaf

Other print options are accessible from within a special dialog. This is launched from within the Print dialog.

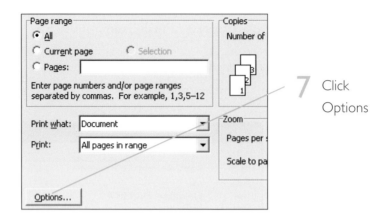

7 Click Options

8 Perform steps 9 thru 13 below, as appropriate

9 Ensure this is checked to print with minimal formatting

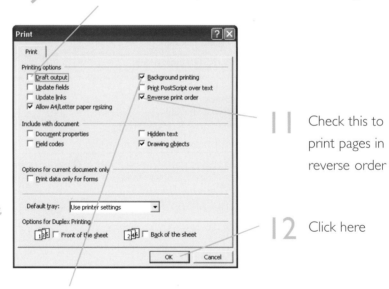

If you want to speed up printing, deselect background printing. The drawback, however, is that you won't be able to continue working until printing is complete.

11 Check this to print pages in reverse order

12 Click here

10 Uncheck this to turn off background printing

13 Follow step 14 on page 97

Excel 2003

Get up-and-running with Excel 2003 in a hurry. Pages 100 thru 112 explain basic techniques like selecting and entering data, Smart Tags and using worksheets. After this, you'll move on rapidly and easily to advanced techniques such as formulas/functions, error checking and cell tracking. You'll also format your worksheets for maximum effect, search for and replace data, insert pictures and convert data into charts. Finally, you'll customize worksheet layout, preview your work and print it.

Covers

Chapter Three

The Excel 2003 screen

Below is a detailed illustration of the Excel 2003 screen:

For further coverage of Excel 2003 features, see a companion title: "Excel 2003 in easy steps".

Formula bar   Column letters

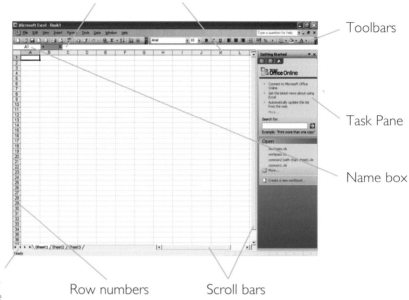

Toolbars

Task Pane

Name box

This is the worksheet Tab area. The screen components here are used to move between Excel worksheets – see page 107.

Row numbers   Scroll bars

Specifying which screen components display

Pull down the Tools menu and click Options. Then:

You can have Excel display formulas (rather than their values) globally within cells. This is a useful feature in moderation. Just check Formulas under Window options.

1 Ensure the View tab is active

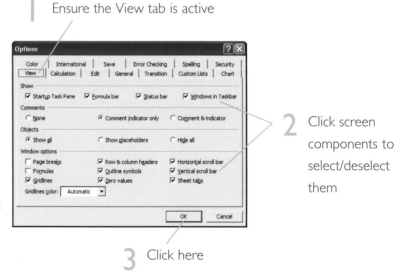

You can also hide sheet tabs, though doing so may possibly decrease worksheet functionality. Uncheck Sheet tabs.

2 Click screen components to select/deselect them

3 Click here

Entering data

Spreadsheets are like word processor documents but they work predominantly with numerical calculations rather than just text.

When you run Excel 2003, you're actually opening a new workbook (see "Beyond cells" below). Excel calls these "Book 1", "Book 2" and so on.

When you start Excel 2003, you're presented with a new blank worksheet (spreadsheet):

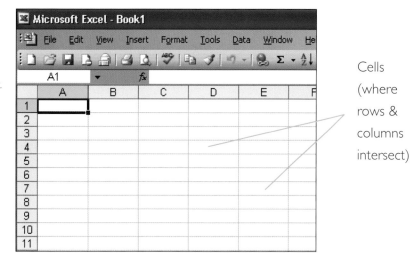

Cells (where rows & columns intersect)

This means that you can start entering data immediately.

In Excel, you can enter the following basic data types:

*   values (numbers) or dates (separate components by - or /) or times (e.g. **6.45 a** for 6.45 a.m. or **3.55 p** for 3.55 p.m.)

*   text (e.g. headings and explanatory material)

*   math functions (e.g. Sine or Cosine)

*   formulas (combinations of values, text and functions)

You enter data into "cells". Cells are formed where rows and columns intersect.

Columns are vertical, rows horizontal. Each worksheet has up to 256 columns and 65,536 rows, making a total of 16,777,216 cells.

Beyond cells

Collections of rows/columns and cells are known in Excel as worksheets. Worksheets are organized into workbooks (by default, each workbook has 3 worksheets). Workbooks are the files that are stored on disk when you save your work in Excel.

When you enter values which are too big (physically) to fit in the holding cell, Excel 2003 may insert an error message.

To resolve this, widen the column. Or pull down the Format menu and click Column, Autofit Selection to have Excel automatically increase the column size to match the contents.

Although you can enter data *directly* into a cell (by simply clicking in the cell and typing it in), there's another method you can use which is often easier. Excel provides a special screen component known as the Formula bar.

The illustration below shows the end of a blank worksheet. Some sample text has been inserted into cell IV65536 (note that the Name box tells you which cell is currently active).

Name box   Formula bar

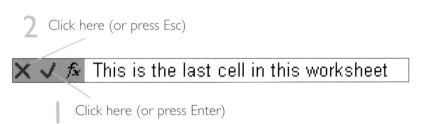

You can enter the same data into more than one cell. Select the cells then type in the data. Hit Ctrl+Enter.

If you start to enter alphanumeric data in a cell and Excel determines that it matches data already present in that column, it fills in the remaining data for you. Hit Enter to accept the suggestion.

Entering data via the Formula bar

Click the cell you want to insert data into. Then click the Formula bar. Type in the data. Then follow step 1 below. If you decide not to proceed with the operation, follow step 2 instead:

2 Click here (or press Esc)

X ✓ fx This is the last cell in this worksheet

Click here (or press Enter)

Modifying existing data

You can amend the contents of a cell in two ways:

You can hide data temporarily, to make your worksheet easier to use. Select one or more rows or columns then choose Format, Row, Hide or Format, Column, Hide.

(To unhide data, choose ...Unhide in the same submenu.)

- via the Formula bar

- from within the cell

When you use either of these methods, Excel 2003 enters a special state known as Edit Mode.

Amending existing data using the Formula bar

Click the cell whose contents you want to change. Then click in the Formula bar. Make the appropriate revisions and/or additions. Then press Enter. Excel updates the relevant cell.

Amending existing data internally

To undo or redo any editing action, press Ctrl+Z or Ctrl+Y.

Click the cell whose contents you want to change. Press F2. Make the appropriate revisions and/or additions *within the cell*. Then press Enter.

The illustration below shows a section from a blank workbook:

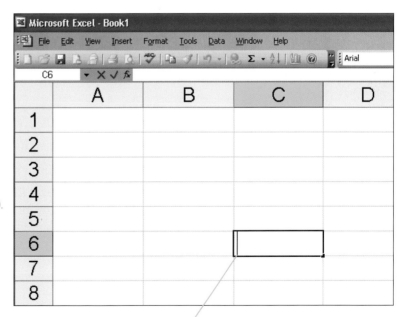

The way Excel actually displays data in cells depends on the number format applied – see page 120.

Also crucial are the Windows XP Regional settings (Control Panel, Regional and Language Options – Regional Options tab).

Cell C6 in Edit Mode (note the flashing insertion point)

Working with cell ranges

When you're working with more than one cell, it's often convenient and useful to organize them in "ranges". A range is a rectangular arrangement of cells. In the illustration below, cells A2, A3, A4, A5, A6, B2, B3, B4, B5 and B6 have been selected:

A selected cell range

This is "relative referencing" – i.e. if you moved the range, Excel would update the reference intelligently. Some cell contents, however, need to be "absolute" – in other words, they don't change. Examples of this would include interest rates that are constant.

To make a reference absolute, just prefix each component with $. For example, if a formula instructed Excel to multiply the contents of E3 (relative) by an interest rate in B1, the formula would be =E3*B1.

This description of cells is very cumbersome. It's much more useful to use a form of shorthand. Excel 2003 (using the start and end cells as reference points) refers to these cells as *A2:B6*.

You can extend this even more. Cell addresses can also incorporate a component which refers to the worksheet that contains the range. For example, to denote that the range A2:B6 is in a worksheet called Sheet8, you'd use: *Sheet8!A2:B6*.

Excel also supports an older, absolute referencing style called "RICI".

RICI works a bit like chessboard notation: R3C6 (row 3, column 6) equates to F3 in normal relative mode.

To use RICI, choose Tools, Options. Hit the General tab and check "RICI reference style".

Additional shortcuts

You can also use additional reference shortcuts (use the following as guides):

All cells in row 15	*15:15*	All cells in column A	*A:A*
All cells in rows 8–20	*8:20*	All cells in columns P–S	*P:S*

Smart Tags

By default, Smart Tags may be disabled. To turn them on, choose Tools, AutoCorrect Options. Select the Smart Tags tab and check Label data with smart tags. Click OK.

Excel 2003 recognizes certain types of data and flags them with a purple triangle in the relevant cell. When you move the mouse pointer over the triangle, an "action button" appears that provides access to commands which would otherwise have to be accessed from menus/toolbars or even other programs. Smart Tags are data-specific labels.

There are several types of Smart Tag in Excel 2003. These include names from your Outlook Contact list or from email recipients and financial symbols.

You can search for and download more Smart Tags from the Web. Choose Tools, AutoCorrect Options. Select the Smart Tags tab and check More Smart Tags. Follow the on-screen instructions.

Using Smart Tags

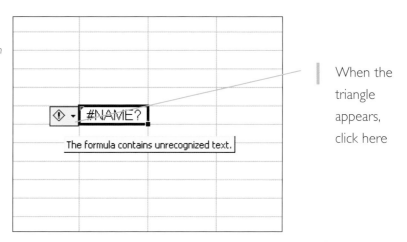

When the triangle appears, click here

Like Word, Excel also gives access to extra action buttons that resemble Smart Tags. These include Paste Options and AutoCorrect – see page 36 for more information.

Other Smart Tags in Excel include financial symbols and Outlook contacts.

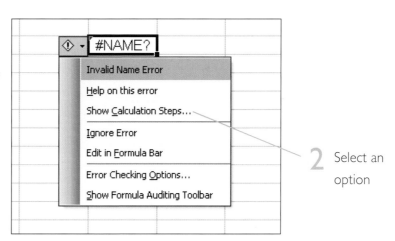

2 Select an option

Moving around in worksheets

Excel 2003 facilitates worksheet navigation. As you move the insertion point from cell to cell, the relevant row and column headers are highlighted.

Using the keyboard

1 Use the cursor keys to move one cell left, right, up or down

2 Hold down Ctrl as you use 1. above; this jumps to the edge of the current section (e.g. if cell B11 is active and you hold down Ctrl as you press the right cursor, Excel jumps to IV11)

3 Press Home to jump to the first cell in the active row, or Ctrl+Home to move to A1

4 Press Page Up or Page Down to move up or down by 1 screen

5 Press Alt+Page Down to move one screen to the right, or Alt+Page Up to move one screen to the left

Using the scroll bar

1 To scroll quickly to another section of the active worksheet, drag the scroll box along the scroll bar until you reach it (hold down Shift to speed it up)

2 To move one window to the left or right, click to the left or right of the scroll box in the horizontal scroll bar

3 To move one window up or down, click above or below the scroll box in the vertical scroll bar

4 To move up or down by one row, click the arrows in the vertical scroll bar

5 To move left or right by one column, click the arrows in the horizontal scroll bar

Using the Go To dialog

1 Hit F5

2 In the Go To dialog, type in a cell reference (its positional identification e.g. H23) or a cell range then click OK

Switching between worksheets

Because workbooks have more than one worksheet, Excel provides two easy and convenient methods for moving between them.

Using the Tab area

You can use the Tab area (at the base of the Excel screen – see page 100) to:

- jump to the first or last sheet

- jump to the next or previous sheet

- jump to a specific sheet

See the illustration below:

When you click a worksheet tab, Excel 2003 emboldens the name and makes the tab background white.

To first sheet   To next sheet   Standard sheet tab

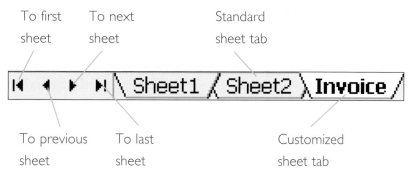

To previous sheet   To last sheet   Customized sheet tab

You can enter or amend data in more than one worksheet at a time: just select multiple worksheet tabs and make the changes. However, don't forget that data may be replaced in the process.

To move to a specific sheet, simply click the relevant tab.

An example: in the illustration above, to jump to the "Invoice" worksheet, simply click the appropriate tab.

Using the keyboard

1   Hit Ctrl+Page Up to move to the previous worksheet tab

2   Hit Ctrl+Page Down to move to the next worksheet tab

Viewing several worksheets

OK, this isn't exactly a high-tech solution but it is a great way to beat a common Excel problem: worksheets becoming so large that it's hard to view the data you need.

(The Watch Window is pretty useful, too – see page 111.)

Excel 2003 also lets you view multiple worksheets simultaneously. This can be particularly useful when they have data in common. Viewing multiple worksheets is a two stage process.

| To open a new window, pull down the Window menu and click New Window

To switch between active windows, pull down the Window menu and click the relevant entry in the list at the bottom. Or hit Ctrl+F6.

Excel tells you you're working with an alternative view by incrementing a number in its title in the menu bar. For example, the worksheet "new" will have "new:1", "new:2" and so on.

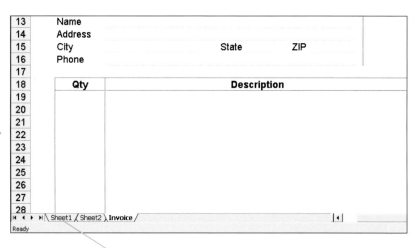

If you want to work with alternative views of the same worksheet – a useful technique in itself – simply omit steps 2–3.

2 Excel now launches a new window showing an alternative view of the active worksheet. Click the relevant sheet tab

3 Repeat step 2 for each new sheet you want to view

4 For best effect, refine the way the windows are arranged – see the facing page

Rearranging worksheet windows

When you have multiple worksheet windows open at once, you can have Excel arrange them in specific patterns. This is useful because it makes worksheets more visible and accessible. Options are:

Tiled   Windows are displayed side by side:

Horizontal   Windows are displayed in a tiled column, with horizontal subdivisions:

Vertical   Windows are displayed in a tiled row, with vertical subdivisions:

Cascade   Windows are overlaid (with a slight offset):

Rearranging windows

Pull down the Window menu and click Arrange. Then:

Checking "Windows of active workbook" only displays sheets in the current workbook.

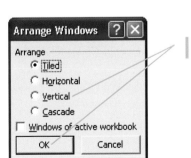

Click an arrangement then select OK

Other operations on worksheets

We said earlier that, by default, each workbook has 3 worksheets. However, you can easily add, delete and move worksheets.

To rearrange worksheets, select 1 or more sheet tabs then drag them to a new location in the Tab area.

Inserting a single worksheet

1. In the worksheet Tab area at the base of the screen, click the tab for the sheet in front of which you want the new worksheet inserted. Pull down the Insert menu and click Worksheet

2. Pull down the Insert menu and click Worksheet. Or hit Shift+F11

To move sheets to another workbook, select 1 or more tabs. Pull down the Edit menu and click Move or Copy Sheet. In the To book field, select a host workbook. Then click the sheet in front of which you want the transferred sheet(s) to appear. Check Create a copy if you want to copy rather than a move operation. Click OK.

Inserting multiple worksheets

1. Select the required number of sheet tabs by Shift-clicking them. Then pull down the Insert menu and click Worksheet

2. Pull down the Insert menu and click Worksheet. Or hit Shift+F11

Deleting worksheets

1. Select one or more worksheet tabs (see above)

2. Pull down the Edit menu and click Delete Sheet

In worksheets that have the same format, you can use 3D referencing in some functions. Use the following syntax as a base:
To add B5 and C8 in Sheets1–3, you'd enter:
=SUM(Sheet1:Sheet3!B5:C8)

3. Click here to proceed with the deletion (the worksheet contents are automatically deleted, too)

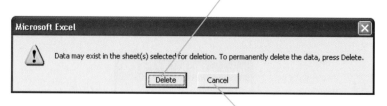

4. Or here to cancel it and return to your workbook

Tracking cells

You can use the Watch Window to track cells (often those containing formulas) while you're working on another part of the same or another sheet, or even in another workbook. The Watch Window stops you having to continually switch between worksheets and workbooks.

Using the Watch Window

1 Select the cell(s) you want to watch

To remove a cell from the Watch Window, select its entry and click Delete Watch.

2 Choose Tools, Formula Auditing, Show Watch Window

3 Click Add Watch

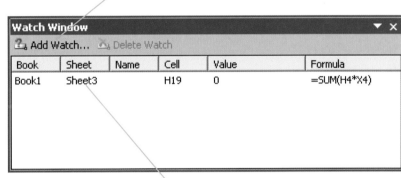

Book	Sheet	Name	Cell	Value	Formula
Book1	Sheet3		H19	0	=SUM(H4*X4)

If the Watch Window has entries that refer to another workbook, they only display if the other workbook is currently open.

5 To view a cell, double-click its entry

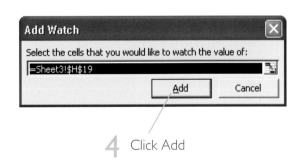

4 Click Add

Selection techniques

You can also use this technique. Place the cell pointer in the first cell. Press F8 – "EXT" appears in the Status bar. Use the cursor keys to define the selection. Finally, press F8 again.

Before you can carry out any editing operations on cells in Excel, you have to select them first. Selecting a single cell is very easy: you merely click in it. However, Excel provides a variety of selection techniques which you can use to select more than one cell.

Selecting adjacent cell ranges

The easiest way to do this is to use the mouse. Click in the first cell in the range; hold down the left mouse button and drag over the remaining cells. Release the mouse button.

To select every cell in a row or column, click the row or column heading. To select multiple rows or columns, click one row or column heading. Drag to select adjacent rows or columns.

You can use the keyboard, too. Select the first cell in the range. Hold down one Shift key as you use the relevant cursor key to extend the selection. Release the keys when the correct selection has been defined.

Selecting separate cell ranges

Excel lets you select more than one range at a time:

Selected ranges (cells, except the first, are see-through, so you can view changes to underlying data)

To select an entire worksheet, press Ctrl+A.

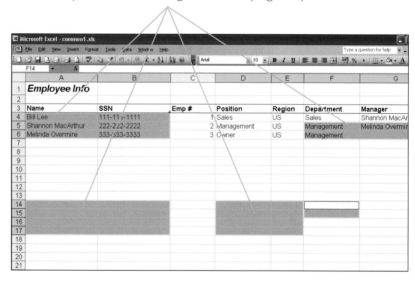

A useful shortcut that needs a bit of practice. Select one or more cell ranges then hold down Shift. Click the last cell you want in the selection – Excel selects all cells between the first selected cell and the one you just clicked.

In the example (and ignoring the selections on the right of the illustration), if you selected A14:B17 first and then selected A4:B6, Shift-clicking B15 would select A4:B17 . . .

To select joint ranges, select the first in the normal way (you can only use the mouse method here). Then hold down Ctrl as you select subsequent ranges.

Formulas – an overview

Formulas are cell entries which define how other values relate to each other.

As a very simple example, consider the following:

The underlying formula – see below

	A	B
1	**Product/Service Catalog**	
2		
3	**Product/Service Name**	**Price**
4	Fine Lamps	$60.00
5	Leather Chairs	$85.00
6	Hardwood Desks	$175.00
7		
8		
9		
10		$320.00

Microsoft Excel - common1.xls

File Edit View Insert Format Tools Data Window Help

B10   *f*x =SUM(B4:B6)

Total

To select cells that contain formulas, pre-select a range (or select a typical cell) then hit F5. Click the Special button and select Formulas. Check the data types you want to select and hit OK.

Here, a cell has been defined which returns the total of cells B4:B6. Obviously, in this instance you could insert the total easily enough yourself because the individual values are so small, and because we're only dealing with a small number of cells. But what happens if the cell values are larger and/or more numerous, or – more to the point – if they're liable to change frequently?

The answer is to insert a formula which carries out the necessary calculation automatically.

If you look at the Formula bar in the illustration, you'll see the formula which does this:

=SUM(B4:B6)

Many Excel formulas are much more complex than this, but the principles remain the same.

Inserting a formula

Arguments (e.g. cell references) relating to functions are always contained in brackets.

All formulas in Excel 2003 begin with an equals sign. This is usually followed by a permutation of the following:

- an operand (cell reference, e.g. B4)

- a function (e.g. the summation function, SUM)

- a math operator (+, –, / and *)

- comparison operators (<, >, <=, >= and =)

Excel supports a very wide range of functions organized into numerous categories. For more information on how to insert functions, see page 116.

The math operators are (in the order in which they appear in the list): *plus, minus, divide* and *multiply.*

The comparison operators are (in the order in which they appear in the list): *less than, greater than, less than or equal to, greater than or equal to* and *equals.*

There are two ways to enter formulas:

Entering a formula directly into the cell

To enter the same formula into a cell range, select the range, type the formula and then press Ctrl+Enter.

1 Click a cell then type = followed by your formula. When you've finished, press Enter

Entering a formula into the Formula bar

1 Click a cell then click in the Formula bar. Type = followed by your formula

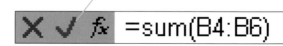

In the formula itself, Excel outlines the cell reference in blue. The cells referenced by the formula are also outlined.

2 When you've finished, press Enter

3 Or click here

Using the Formula Evaluator

You can only evaluate one cell at a time.

When formulas become complex (as they frequently do), it can be difficult to see how Excel arrives at the eventual result. However, you can use a feature called Formula Evaluator to step through each calculation.

Excel produces error messages (with Smart Tags) when it doesn't understand what you enter. Common messages include:

- *#NAME? – usually refers to unrecognized functions*
- *#DIV/0 – you've tried to divide a number by 0 (zero)*
- *#N/A – usually means your function is referencing the wrong type of content*
- *###### – the number in the cell is too long*
- *#NUM! – indicates problems with numbers (e.g. trying to return 100^{1000})*

1 Select the cell which contains the formula. Pull down the Tools menu and click Formula Auditing, Evaluate Formula

3 Click Step In to view a linked formula or Step Out to return to the original

5 Click Restart to begin over

4 Click Close

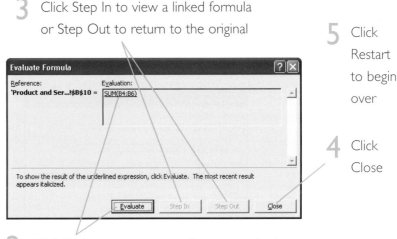

2 Click Evaluate – repeat as often as required

Using the Formula Auditing toolbar

Precedents are cells referenced to by formulas in other cells. Dependents are cells with formulas which reference other cells.

Error checking is very useful. If you hit any problems, select Help on this error.

1 Choose View, Toolbars, Show Formula Auditing Toolbar then:

Error checking

Show/hide dependents

Launch Formula Evaluator

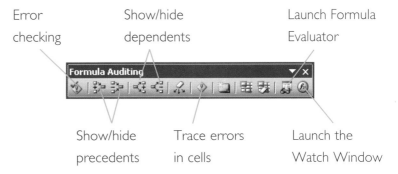

Show/hide precedents

Trace errors in cells

Launch the Watch Window

Inserting a function

Functions are pre-defined tools which accomplish specific tasks. These tasks are often calculations; occasionally, however, they're more generalized (e.g. some functions simply return dates and/or times). In effect, functions replace one or more formulas.

Functions can only be used in formulas.

Excel 2003 organizes its functions under convenient headings e.g. Financial, Date & Time or Statistical.

If you invoke this process after you've already typed in part of the formula, omit steps 2–4.

1 Just after you've typed = refer to the Formula bar and click this button: ƒx

2 Type in a brief description of the function you want and click here

3 Or select a category

Want help with using a function? Click here:

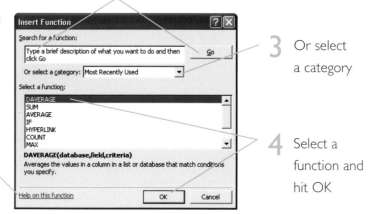

4 Select a function and hit OK

5 Enter the function arguments

If you know the function you want and it's fairly simple, you can enter it directly into a cell (preceded by =). When you do this, Excel often launches a helpful tip.

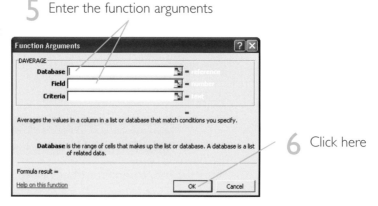

6 Click here

Amending row/column sizes

You can also use a dialog. Select rows or columns then choose Format, Column, Width or Format, Row, Height.

Sooner or later, when there is too much data in cells to display adequately, you'll find it necessary to resize rows or columns.

Changing row height

Want to have one column's width match another? Click in the column you want to copy and hit Ctrl+C. Select the target column and choose Edit, Paste Special. In the dialog, select Column widths and hit OK.

1 To change one row's height, click the row heading. If you want to change multiple rows, hold down Ctrl and click the appropriate extra headings

2 Place the mouse pointer (it changes to a cross) just under the row heading(s) and drag up or down

Excel has a useful "Best Fit" feature. When the mouse pointer has changed to the form shown in the illustration, double-click to have the row(s) or column(s) adjust themselves automatically to their contents.

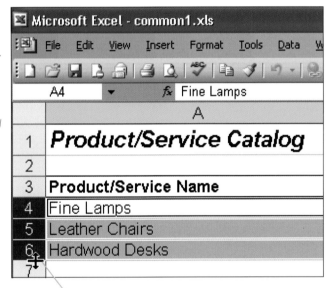

The transformed pointer. Rows 4–6 are being amended

Changing column width

To set a standard column width for all sheets in the active workbook, right-click a sheet tab and hit Select All Sheets. Choose Format, Column, Standard Width. Set a width in the dialog.

1 Follow step 1 above but select one or more column headings

2 Place the mouse pointer (it changes to a cross) to the right of the column heading(s) and drag to the left or right

Inserting cells, rows or columns

You can insert additional cells, rows or columns into worksheets.

If you select cells in more than one row or column, Excel 2003 inserts the equivalent number of new rows or columns.

Inserting a new row or column

First, select one or more cells within the row(s) or column(s) where you want to carry out the insert operation. Now pull down the Insert menu and click Rows or Columns, as appropriate. Excel 2003 inserts the new row(s) or column(s) immediately.

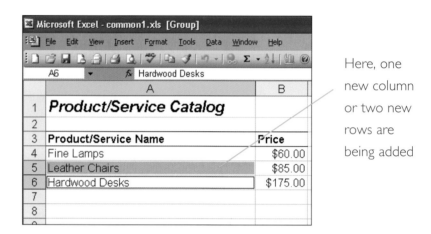

Here, one new column or two new rows are being added

Inserting a new cell range

Select the range where you want to insert the new cells. Pull down the Insert menu and click Cells. Now carry out step 1 or step 2 below. Finally, follow step 3.

1 Click here to have Excel make room for the new cells by moving the selected range *to the right*

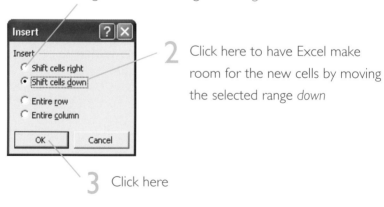

2 Click here to have Excel make room for the new cells by moving the selected range *down*

3 Click here

AutoFill

Excel 2003 lets you insert data series automatically. This is a very useful and timesaving feature. Look at the illustration below:

- *1st Period, 2nd Period, 3rd Period etc.*
- *Mon, Tue, Wed etc.*
- *Quarter 1, Quarter 2, Quarter 3 etc.*
- *Week1, Week2, Week3 etc.*

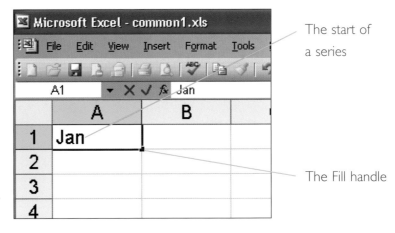

The start of a series

The Fill handle

If you wanted to insert month names in successive cells in column A, you could do so manually. But there's a much easier way. You can use Excel's AutoFill feature.

Using AutoFill to create a series

Data series don't need to contain every possibility. For instance, you could have: "Mon, Thu, Sun, Wed" etc.

1 Type in the first element(s) of the series in consecutive cells then select all the cells

2 Drag the fill handle over the cells into which you want to extend the series (in the example above, A2:A12) – Excel 2003 extrapolates the initial entry or entries into the appropriate series

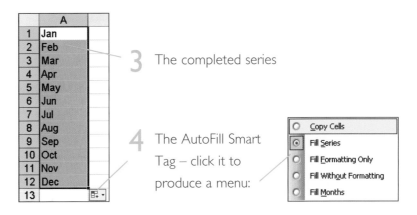

3 The completed series

4 The AutoFill Smart Tag – click it to produce a menu:

Changing number formats

Excel 2003 lets you insert and work with Euros. To insert the Euro symbol: €
hold down Alt and press 0128 on the Numerical keypad. Finally, release the Alt key.

Fonts which support Euros include: Courier, Tahoma, Times and Arial.

Excel 2003 lets you apply formatting enhancements to cells and their contents. You can:

- specify a number format

- customize the font, type size and style of contents

- specify cell alignment

- border and/or shade cells

Specifying a number format

You can customize the way cell contents (e.g. numbers and dates/times) display in Excel. For example, you can specify at what point numbers are rounded up. Available formats are organized under several general categories. These include: Number, Accounting and Fraction.

You can create your own number formats. Select Custom in the Category list then apply the formatting you want.

1 Select the cells whose contents you want to customize then hit Ctrl+I

2 Ensure the Number tab is active

Sometimes, you likely will want to enter numbers as text (e.g. a telephone or Social Security number). In this case, choose the Text category.

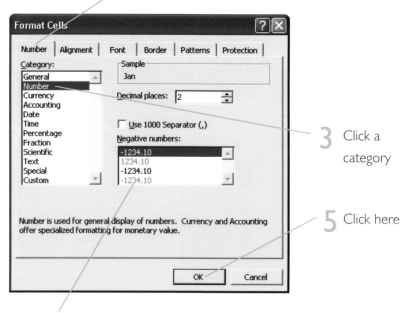

3 Click a category

If a cell has had the Date number format applied, dates appear by default in a specific format. For example, "August 12, 2003" is shown as: 8/12/2003.

To change this, specify a new format in step 4.

5 Click here

4 Complete these options (they vary with the category)

Changing fonts and styles

Excel lets you carry out the following actions on cell contents (numbers and/or text). You can:

- apply a new font and/or type size

- apply a font style (for most fonts, you can choose from: Regular, Italic, Bold or Bold Italic)

- apply a color

- apply a special effect: underlining, ~~strikethrough~~, superscript or subscript

Amending the appearance of cell contents

Don't overdo formatting changes; use them in moderation, to make your worksheets more impactful.

| Select the cells you want to format then hit Ctrl+1

2 Carry out step 3 below. Now follow any of steps 4–7, as appropriate. Finally, carry out step 8

Check Normal Font to apply the default formatting.

3 Ensure the Font tab is active

5 Type in a type size

To apply underlining, click the arrow to the right of the Underline box and select an underlining type.

6 Specify a color

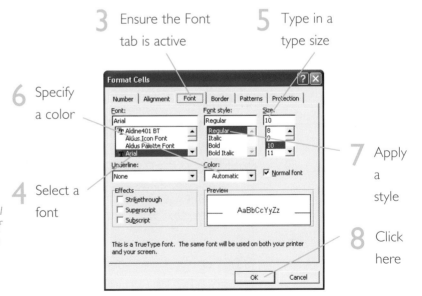

4 Select a font

7 Apply a style

8 Click here

To apply a special effect, click any of the options in the Effects section.

Cell alignment and text wrap

By default, Excel aligns text to the left of cells, and numbers to the right. However, you can change this and other alignment aspects.

Check Shrink to fit to make text look smaller so it fits within its column.

1 Select the cell(s) whose contents you want to realign then hit Ctrl+1

2 Ensure the Alignment tab is active

Check Merge cells to combine multiple pre-selected cells into one (their new reference is that of the original upper left cell).

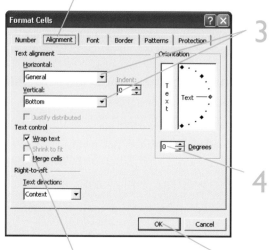

3 Select vertical and horizontal alignments and, optionally, insert a value in Indent to indent cell contents (by character widths)

4 Enter a rotation angle

You can amend rotation (the direction of text flow within cells) by specifying a plus (anticlockwise) or minus (clockwise) angle.

5 Check this to wrap text – see below

6 Click here

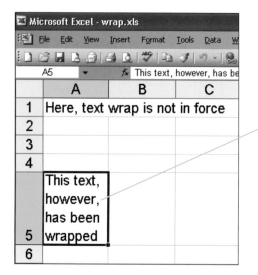

Text wrap forces surplus text onto separate lines within the host cell (instead of overflowing into adjacent cells to the right) and makes text look neater and easier to follow

Bordering cells

Excel 2003 lets you define a border around:

- the perimeter of a selected cell range

- specific sides within a cell range

You can customize the border by choosing from a selection of pre-defined border styles. You can also add new line styles to specific sides, or color the border.

You can also border by hand. In the Borders toolbar (View, Toolbars, Borders), set the style and color. Then click this button:

and drag out a border.

Applying a cell border

1 Select the cells you want to border then hit Ctrl+1

2 Carry out step 3 below. Follow step 4 to apply an overall border. Carry out step 5 if you want to deactivate one or more border sides. Perform step 6 if you want to color the border. Finally, carry out step 7:

3 Ensure the Border tab is active

If you want to customize the border style, apply a line style from the Style section just before step 4.

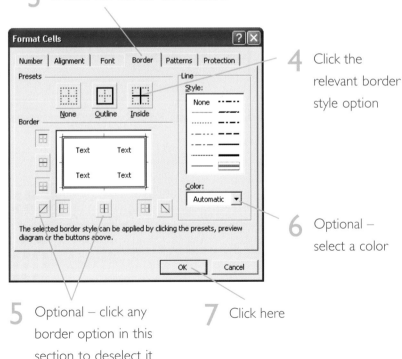

4 Click the relevant border style option

6 Optional – select a color

5 Optional – click any border option in this section to deselect it

7 Click here

Shading cells

You can only apply a foreground color if you apply a foreground pattern as well.

Excel 2003 lets you apply a background color, a foreground pattern or a foreground color to cells. Interesting effects can be achieved by using pattern and color combinations with colored backgrounds.

Applying a pattern or background

First, select the cell range you want to shade. Pull down the Format menu and click Cells. Now carry out step 1. Perform step 2 to apply a *background* color, and/or 3–5 to apply a *foreground* pattern or a pattern/color combination. Finally, follow step 6.

1 | Ensure the Patterns tab is active

Use this handy shortcut. When you want to apply the most recently used color, click this button on the Formatting toolbar:

Or click the arrow and select another color in the list. (To remove a fill, hit No Fill instead.)

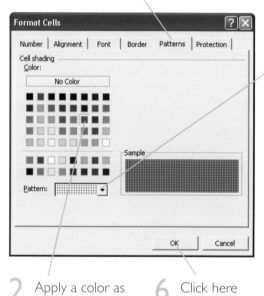

3 Click here to apply a foreground pattern or a pattern/color combination

Use borders, colors and patterns to distinguish between different types of information and thus make your worksheets easier to understand.

2 Apply a color as a background

6 Click here

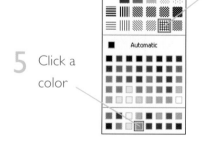

4 Click a pattern

5 Click a color

AutoFormat

Excel 2003 provides a shortcut to the formatting of worksheet data: AutoFormat. AutoFormat consists of some 16 pre-defined formatting schemes. These incorporate specific excerpts from the font, number, alignment, border and shading options discussed earlier. You can apply any of these schemes to selected cell ranges with just a few mouse clicks. You can even specify which scheme elements you *don't* wish to use.

AutoFormat works with most arrangements of worksheet data.

Using AutoFormat

1 Select the cells (more than one) you want to format then choose Format, AutoFormat

To remove an AutoFormat, select the None format at the bottom of the list.

Format cell ranges or series (lists) with AutoFormat.

2 Select an AutoFormat

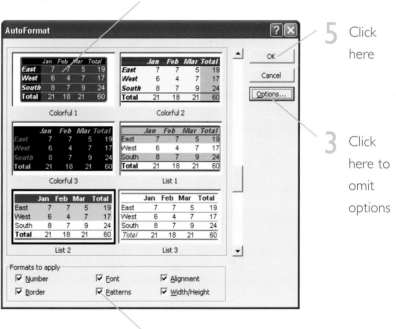

5 Click here

3 Click here to omit options

4 If you followed step 3, uncheck options you don't want to use

The Format Painter

Excel 2003 provides a very useful tool which can save you a lot of time and effort: the Format Painter. You can use the Format Painter to copy the formatting attributes from cells you've previously formatted to other cells, in one operation.

Using the Format Painter

1 Apply the necessary formatting, if you haven't already done so. Then select the formatted cells

Duuble-click the Format Painter icon if you want to apply the selected formatting more than once. Then repeat step 3 as often as necessary.

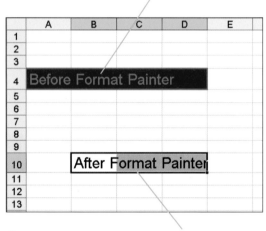

2 Refer to the Standard toolbar and click this icon:

You can also use Format Painter with "objects" (e.g. pictures or clip art).

3 Select the cell(s) you want the formatting copied to

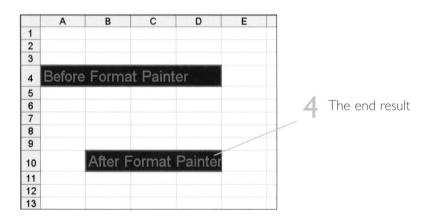

4 The end result

5 Press Esc when you've finished using Format Painter

Find operations

You can use wildcards in your searches (but not in replace operations).
However, the only Excel wildcards are:

• *?* stands for any one character

• *** stands for any number of characters

• *~ prefix this to ? or * (if you want to search for these characters rather than use them as wildcards)*

Excel 2003 lets you search for and jump to text or numbers (in short, any information) in your worksheets. This is a particularly useful feature when worksheets become large and complex.

You can organize your search by rows or by columns. You can also specify whether Excel looks in:

• cells that contain formulas – **follow step 3 and select Formulas in the Look in box**

• cells that don't contain formulas – **follow step 3 and select Values in the Look in box**

Additionally, you can insist that Excel only flag exact matches (i.e. if you searched for "11", Excel would not find "1111"), and you can also limit text searches to text which has the case you specified (e.g. searching for "PRODUCT LIST" would not find "Product List" or "product list").

Searching for data

To search for data over more than one worksheet, select the relevant sheet tabs before launching the Find dialog box.

| To search the entire worksheet, hit Ctrl+F

If you want to restrict the search to specific cells, select a cell range before you launch the Find dialog.

2 Type in the data you want to find

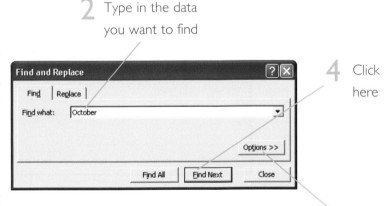

4 Click here

You can also search for specific formatting (such as typefaces, alignments and borders). After step 3, click Format and complete the Find Format dialog.

3 To specify the search direction, limit it to certain cell types or make it case-specific, click Options and complete the dialog which appears

Find-and-replace operations

When you search for data, you can also have Excel 2003 replace it with something else.

Find-and-replace operations can be organized by rows or columns. However, unlike straight searches, you can't specify whether Excel looks in cells that contain formulas or not. As with straight searches, you can, however, limit find-and-replace operations to exact matches and also (in the case of text) to precise case matches.

Normally, find-and-replace operations only affect the host worksheet. If you want to carry out an operation over multiple worksheets, pre-select the relevant sheet tabs.

Running a find-and-replace operation

1 Select a range if you want to restrict the operation to this

2 Hit Ctrl+H

3 Type in the data you want to find

4 Type in replacement data

5 To set options (see step 3 on page 127) click here

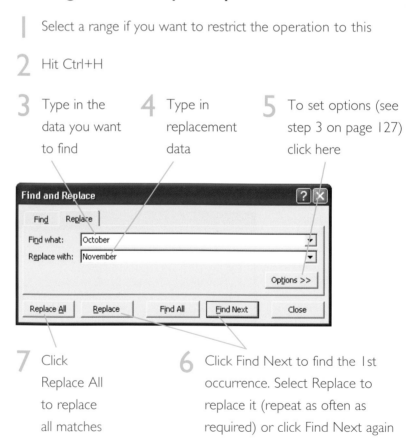

7 Click Replace All to replace all matches

6 Click Find Next to find the 1st occurrence. Select Replace to replace it (repeat as often as required) or click Find Next again

Proofing and research

You can spell- (but not grammar-) check your worksheets. You can also search for synonyms, translate text and carry out research.

You can't spell-check on-the-fly with Excel.

To set spelling options, choose Tools, Options and hit the Spelling tab.

Carrying out a spell-check

| Hit F7

2 Complete the Spelling dialog (spell-checking is basically the same as in Word – see page 77)

Using the Research Pane

| Ctrl+left-click anywhere to launch the Research Pane

2 Enter a word or phrase

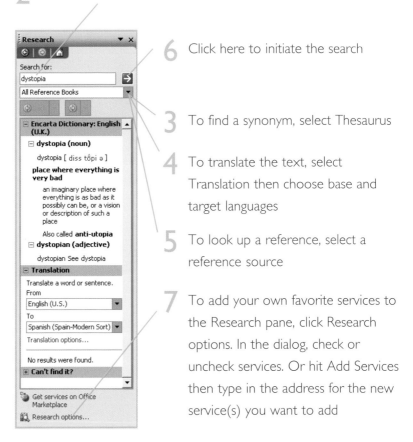

6 Click here to initiate the search

3 To find a synonym, select Thesaurus

4 To translate the text, select Translation then choose base and target languages

5 To look up a reference, select a reference source

7 To add your own favorite services to the Research pane, click Research options. In the dialog, check or uncheck services. Or hit Add Services then type in the address for the new service(s) you want to add

Charting – an overview

Excel 2003 has comprehensive charting capabilities. You can have it convert selected data into its visual equivalent. To do this, Excel offers a wide number of chart formats and sub-formats.

You can create a chart:

- as a picture within the parent worksheet

- as a separate chart sheet (these have their own tabs in the Tab area and these operate just like worksheet tabs)

Excel uses a special Wizard – the Chart Wizard – to make the process of creating charts easy and convenient.

A sample 3-D Area chart:

You can add a picture to chart walls. See page 134

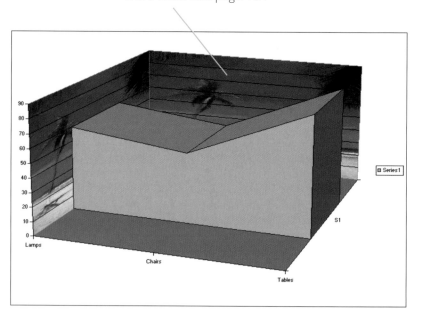

Creating a chart

First, select the cells you want converted into a chart. Pull down the Insert menu and click Chart. The first Chart Wizard dialog appears. Do the following:

Click a chart type

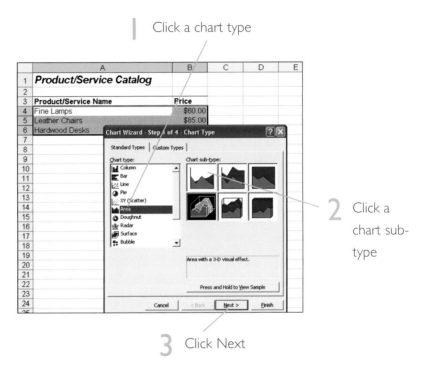

2 Click a chart sub-type

3 Click Next

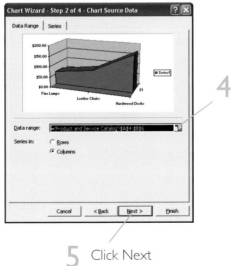

4 If you selected the wrong cells before launching the Wizard, click here to hide the dialog. Select another cell range then click:

5 Click Next

Click any of the additional tabs to set further self-explanatory chart options. For example, activate the Gridlines tab to specify how and where gridlines display...

6 Optional – name the chart and/or axes

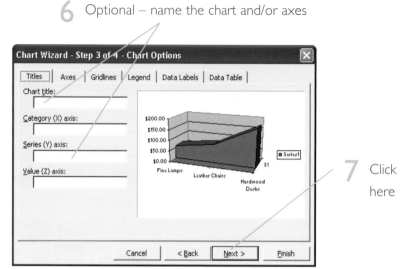

7 Click here

In the final dialog, you tell Excel whether you want the chart inserted into the current worksheet, or into a new chart sheet.

Carry out step 8 OR 9 below. Finally, perform step 10.

8 Click here to create a chart sheet

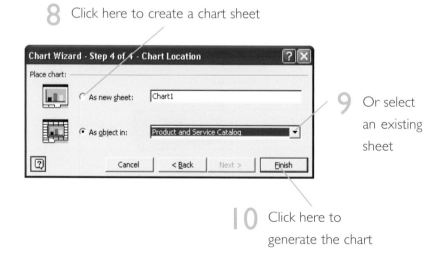

9 Or select an existing sheet

10 Click here to generate the chart

Inserting pictures

Inserting pictures via the Clip Art Task Pane

1 Click where you want to insert the picture

2 Select Insert, Picture, Clip Art

3 Enter one or more keywords (these help you find clips)

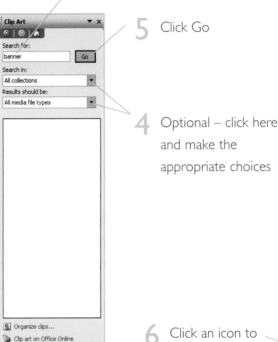

5 Click Go

4 Optional – click here and make the appropriate choices

To add new clips to collections (or add new keywords to existing clips), click the Clip Organizer link at the base of the Task Pane.

6 Click an icon to insert the clip

7 Want more clips? Click Clip art on Office Online for access to a wide variety (and a lot more besides)

Inserting pictures – the dialog route

Once inserted into a worksheet, pictures can be resized and moved in the normal way.

1 Position the insertion point at the location within the active worksheet where you want to insert the picture

2 Select Insert, Picture, From File

4 Click here. In the drop-down list, click the drive/folder that hosts the picture

You can insert pictures or clips onto chart walls. First, select the chart wall then follow the procedures described here or on page 133.

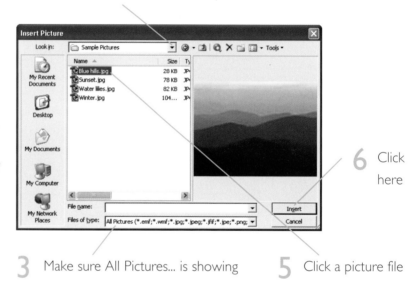

6 Click here

3 Make sure All Pictures... is showing

5 Click a picture file

Inserting pictures via scanners or cameras

Want to customize the acquisition? Click Custom Insert instead then complete your device's dialog.

1 Select Insert, Picture, From Scanner or Camera

You can only import from TWAIN-compliant devices.

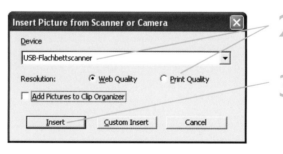

2 Select a device and resolution

3 Click Insert to start the acquisition

Page setup – an overview

Ensuring your worksheets print with the correct page setup can be a complex issue because, with the passage of time, worksheets become so large that they won't fit onto a single page.

You can customize a wide variety of page setup features. These include the paper size and orientation, the scale, the start page number and which worksheet components print. You can also set the standard margin settings.

Page Break Preview

Excel 2003 has a special view mode – Page Break Preview – which you can use to ensure your worksheet prints correctly.

1 Pull down the View menu and click Page Break Preview

Page breaks you've inserted display as solid lines; breaks which Excel has inserted show as dotted lines.

To insert a manual page break, select the row or column immediately to the right of where you want the vertical or horizontal break to appear. Right-click and select Insert Page Break.

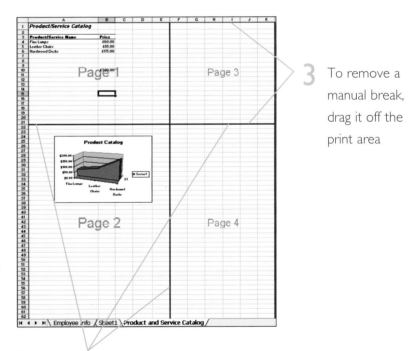

3 To remove a manual break, drag it off the print area

2 Drag page break margins to customize the printable area

4 To leave Page Break Preview, click Normal in the View menu

Setting page options

Excel 2003 comes with 17 pre-defined paper sizes which you can apply to your worksheets, in either portrait (top-to-bottom) or landscape (sideways on) orientation. This is one approach to effective printing. Another is scaling: you can print out your worksheets as they are, or you can have Excel shrink them so that they fit a given paper size (you can even automate this process). Additionally, you can set the print resolution and starting page number.

1 Choose File, Page Setup

2 Ensure the Page tab is active

3 Click the orientation you need

4 Select a page size

To make your worksheet print in a specific number of pages, complete the "Fit to" fields.

Select a print resolution in the Print quality box. This is measured in "dpi" (dots per inch) and is printer-specific.

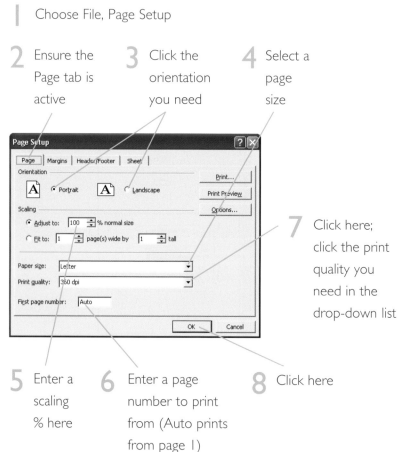

7 Click here; click the print quality you need in the drop-down list

5 Enter a scaling % here

6 Enter a page number to print from (Auto prints from page 1)

8 Click here

Setting margin options

Excel 2003 lets you set a variety of margin settings:

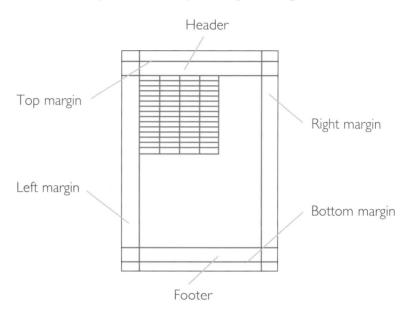

Header

Top margin

Right margin

Left margin

Bottom margin

Footer

1 Choose File, Page Setup

2 Ensure the Margins tab is active

Enter values in the Header and Footer boxes to specify the distance to the top and bottom of the page respectively – these values should always be less than the Top and Bottom margin settings.

To specify how your worksheet aligns on the page, select an option under Center on page.

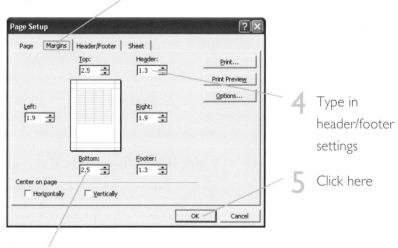

4 Type in header/footer settings

5 Click here

3 Type in the margin settings you need (they're previewed above)

Setting header/footer options

Excel 2003 provides a list of built-in header and footer settings. These settings include the title, the page number, the user's name or "Confidential".

1 Choose File, Page Setup

2 Ensure the Header/ Footer tab is active

3 Click here; select a header from the list

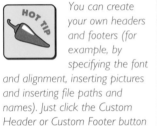

You can create your own headers and footers (for example, by specifying the font and alignment, inserting pictures and inserting file paths and names). Just click the Custom Header or Custom Footer button and complete the dialog.

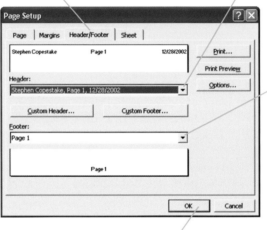

4 Click here; select a footer from the list

5 Click here

Headers and footers are only visible when printed or viewed in Print Preview.

6 One of the stock headers, viewed in Print Preview

Worksheet Functions   Confidential   Page 1

Worksheet Functions Examples

This worksheet contains sample formulas you can use to complete common spreadsheet tasks. Cells containing formulas are blue. To view a sample formula, hover your mouse cursor over the cell to display the comment. Or, press CTRL+` to switch between displaying values and displaying formulas on the worksheet. For more information about a worksheet function, select the cell containing the function, then click the Edit Formula (=) button on the Formula bar.

Suppressing the Display of Error Values

It is common for worksheet formulas to return an error value (#DIV/0!, #N/A, #VALUE!, #REF!, and #NUM!) if they are based on an unexpected value. An example is a simple division formula. If the source cell contains a zero, and #DIV/0! Error will be returned.

Setting sheet options

Excel 2003 lets you:

- define a printable area on-screen

- define a column or row title which will print on every page

- specify which worksheet components should print

- print with minimal formatting

- determine the print direction

Using the Sheet tab in the Page Setup dialog

You can print gridlines if you want – this may make data more readable.

If you want to print a specific cell range (print area), type in the address in the Print area field. Or click the box to the right of the Print area field and drag out a cell selection.

Click Draft quality for rapid printing with the minimum of formatting.

1   Choose File, Page Setup

4   Include or exclude components

2   Select the Sheet tab

5   Type in the address of the row/column you want to use as a consistent title

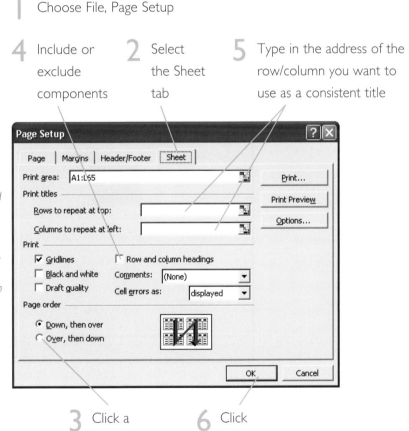

3   Click a direction option

6   Click here

Page setup for charts

Most page setup issues for charts in chart sheets are identical to those for worksheet data. The main difference, however, is that the Page Setup dialog has a Chart (rather than a Sheet) tab.

In the Chart tab, you can opt to have the chart:

- printed at full size

- scaled to fit the page

- user-defined

You can also set the print quality.

Using the Chart tab in the Page Setup dialog

1 Select a chart or chart tab then choose File, Page Setup

2 Ensure the Chart tab is active

Clicking Custom ensures that, when you return to the chart sheet, the chart size can be adjusted with the mouse in the normal way. The chart then prints at whatever size you set.

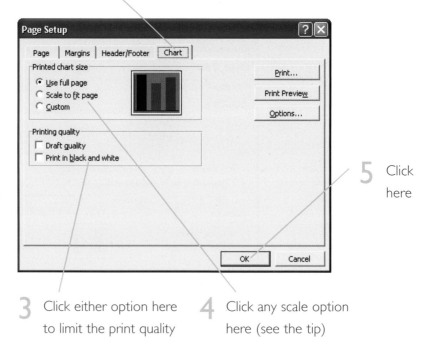

5 Click here

3 Click either option here to limit the print quality

4 Click any scale option here (see the tip)

Launching Print Preview

You can use a special view mode called Print Preview. This displays the active worksheet exactly as it will look when printed. Use Print Preview as a final check just before printing.

1. Pull down the File menu and click Print Preview

Print Preview toolbar

Excel's Print Preview mode only has two Zoom settings: Full Page and High-Magnification.

There are fewer toolbar options if you're previewing a chart.

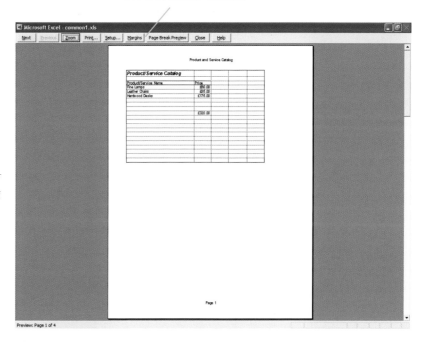

2. To zoom in or out, hit the toolbar Zoom button. Repeat to return to normal

3. Hit Setup in the toolbar to launch the Page Setup dialog

4. Hit Margins in the toolbar then reposition the on-screen margins

5. Hit Page Break Preview in the toolbar to see current breaks

6. Hit Next or Previous in the toolbar to view the succeeding or preceding page

Printing worksheet data

Excel 2003 lets you specify:

- the number of copies you want printed

- whether you want the copies "collated" (for a description, see page 96)

- which pages (or page ranges) you want printed

- whether you want the print run restricted to cells you selected before initiating printing

You can print out your work with the current settings applying. This is a useful shortcut for proofing purposes. Just click this icon in the Standard toolbar:

Starting a print run

1 Select one or more worksheet tabs

2 Optionally, pre-select one or more cell ranges

3 Hit Ctrl+P

7 Type in a page range

4 Select a printer

6 Type in the number of copies required

To adjust your printer's internal settings before you initiate printing, click Properties then refer to your printer's manual.

Print

Printer

Name: Epson Stylus COLOR ESC/P 2 — Properties...

Status: Idle

Type: Epson Stylus COLOR ESC/P 2

Where: LPT1:

Comment: ☐ Print to file

Find Printer...

Print range
- ⦿ All
- ○ Page(s) From: [ ] To: [ ]

Copies

Number of copies: [1]

☑ Collate

Print what
- ○ Selection
- ⦿ Active sheet(s)
- ○ Entire workbook

Preview   OK   Cancel

5 Click the correct selection option

9 Click here

8 Check this to turn on collation

Outlook 2003

This chapter explores the standalone use of Outlook 2003. You'll use the Navigation Pane to launch any of Outlook's associated folders then enter appointments, events, tasks and contact details which Outlook 2003 will now coordinate so that you can manage your business/personal affairs more easily. You'll also use Outlook 2003 to compose, transmit, receive and reply to email, using (optionally) Word 2003 as your editor and working with multiple accounts.

Finally, you'll housekeep your mail and surf the Internet directly from within Outlook 2003.

Covers

Chapter Four

The Outlook 2003 screen

*This view (Mail/
Personal Folders)
is Outlook Today
– a handy starting
point for your use
of Outlook because it provides a
summary of mail, tasks and
appointments.*

*You can specify precisely how
Outlook Today looks and acts –
just click Customize Outlook
Today and complete the options.*

Below is a detailed illustration of a typical Outlook 2003 screen:

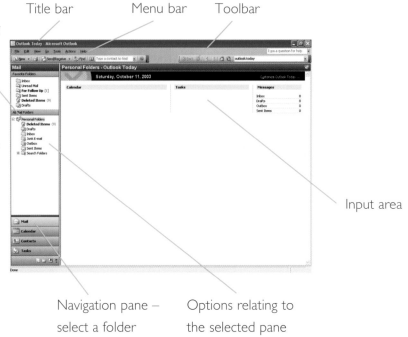

Title bar   Menu bar   Toolbar

Input area

Navigation pane –
select a folder

Options relating to
the selected pane

*To print out work
you do in any
Outlook
component, hit
Ctrl+P. Complete
the Print dialog as normal. In
particular, select a print style –
the choices vary with the pane
selected.*

You can specify which of the four available toolbars display:

Specifying which toolbars display

Pull down the View menu and do the following:

*In this book,
coverage of
Outlook 2003 is
restricted to its
standalone
functions. For information on
group/sharing options, see
"Outlook 2003 in easy steps".*

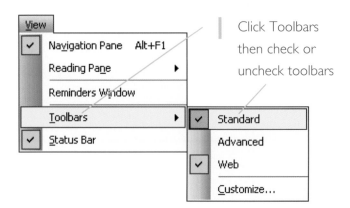

Click Toolbars
then check or
uncheck toolbars

The Navigation Pane

The Navigation Pane gives you access to just about every Outlook feature. You can use it to access the main program panes/areas:

Mail

Use this to store and compose emails. Also provides access to numerous folders such as Inbox, Sent Items, Outbox and Deleted Items

Calendar

Use this to schedule events, tasks, appointments and meetings

Contacts

Use this to manage your business and personal contacts

Want to hide the Navigation Pane? Hit Alt+F1. Repeat to reverse.

Tasks

Enter tasks so you can monitor your progress in completing them

Using the Navigation Pane

Sharing is beyond the scope of this book but you can also open shared contacts or tasks or view other people's shared calendars – just click the appropriate link in step 2.

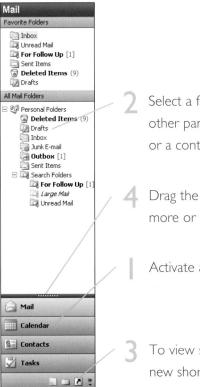

2 Select a folder in the Mail pane (in other panes, select a month/date or a contact/task format)

4 Drag the splitter bar to view more or fewer buttons

Don't like the Navigation Pane as it stands? You can easily customize it. Click the chevron at the base. Select Add or Remove Buttons then click a button. Or to change button order, select Navigation Pane Options then reorder the buttons.

1 Activate a pane

3 To view shortcuts, click here – to add new shortcuts, hit Add New Shortcut

The Calendar – an overview

The Calendar provides alternative ways of viewing and interacting with your schedules. The main views are:

Day/Week/Month

The all-purpose view. An aspect of the Appointment Book; used to enter appointments, events and tasks. You can specify whether you work in the Day, Work Week, Week or Month aspects. (Work Week view stresses the five days of the working week.)

Active Appointments

An aspect of the Appointment Book; used to enter and monitor active appointments

Events

An aspect of the Appointment Book, useful for entering and monitoring events

Active Appointments and Events views give you a handy overview. Just double-click an item to view or edit it or hit Ctrl+N to enter a new item.

To switch to Active Appointments or Events views, choose View, Arrange By, Current View. Select Active Appointments or Events

Switching between the Day, Work Week, Week and Month Calendars

You'll probably use the Day/Week/Month view more than any other because it offers great flexibility. By default, this view displays appointments etc. with the use of the Day aspect. To change the aspect, carry out the following in the Standard toolbar:

To customize what buttons toolbars contain or how big they are, right-click any toolbar and select Customize.

2   Takes you to the current date

Click a view aspect

Using the Day Calendar

You can add appointments to the Day Calendar. If you want, you can stipulate that the appointment is recurring (i.e. it's automatically entered at an interval you specify).

> To launch Day view, click the Day button in step 1 on page 146

Working with appointments in the Day Calendar

Carry out steps 1, 2 and 3 below (then follow step 4 if you want to mark the appointment as recurring):

2 Select a month/day in the Date Navigator

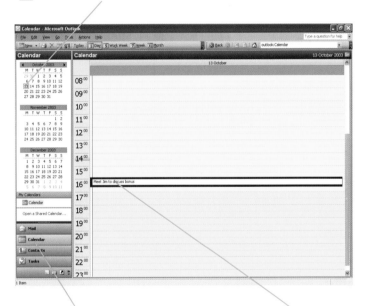

1 Select Calendar in the Navigation Pane

3 Click the relevant time slot; then enter a new appointment by typing in its details and pressing Enter

4 To edit an appointment, double-click it in the Calendar then complete the dialog. For example, to mark a meeting as recurring, click the Recurrence button then set the relevant options

You can add events to the Daily Calendar. Outlook 2003 handles events in a rather different way to appointments. For example, they don't occupy specific time slots in your Appointment Book. Instead, they can relate to any day and can even extend over more than one.

Outlook 2003 distinguishes between events and annual events. Annual events occur yearly on a specific date. Examples of annual events include birthdays/anniversaries while events include seminars and conferences.

Events display as buttons within the Appointment Book.

To amend an existing event, double-click its button.

Adding an event to the Day Calendar

Pull down the Actions menu and click New All Day Event. Now do the following:

4 Click here   2 Enter a description

Type in start and end dates

3 To mark an event as annual or recurring, click Recurrence in the toolbar. In the dialog, complete any further options. Click OK

Using the Week Calendars

You have to use a slightly different process to add appointments. Hit Ctrl+N then carry out the procedures on page 152.

Use the Work Week or Week views as an alternative way to display your appointments and events.

In the Week Calendars, you can enter events and appointments. Enter events using the same procedures as for Day view. For appointments, see the HOT TIP.

To launch a Week view, click the Work Week or Week buttons in step 1 on page 146

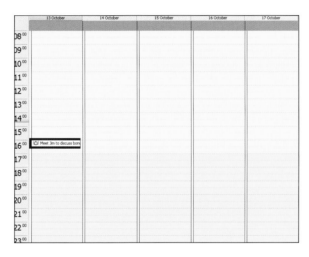

Work Week view – use it to organize your working week

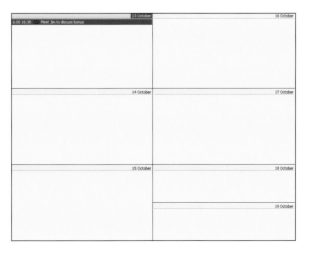

Week view – provides an overview as well as appointment details etc.

Moving around in the Week Calendars

1 Hit Ctrl+G

2 Carry out steps 1–3 and 6 to jump to a specific date in the Week Calendars, or 4–6 as an alternative way to switch between views:

3 Click here

8 Click here

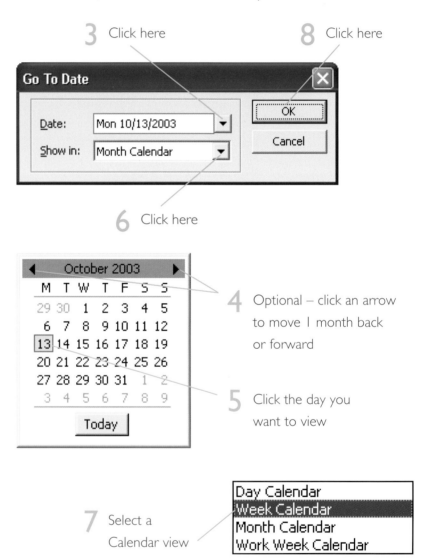

6 Click here

4 Optional – click an arrow to move 1 month back or forward

5 Click the day you want to view

7 Select a Calendar view

Using the Month Calendar

1 To launch Month view, click Month in step 1 on page 146

2 Use the Month Calendar to gain a useful overview of your schedule:

You can use the Find tool to locate specific data. If the Find tool isn't already displaying at the top of the screen, press Ctrl+E. Enter search data and click Find Now. Any matches are shown below the Find window.

Or hit Ctrl+Shift+F for more detailed searches.

Today shows with a colored bar   Event

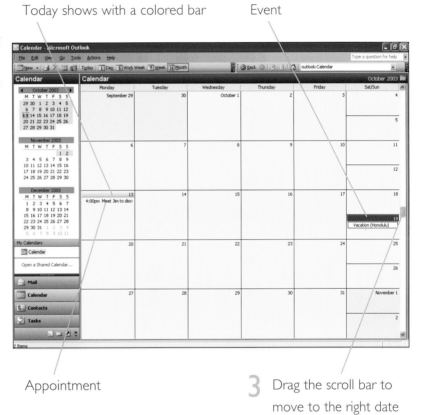

Appointment

3 Drag the scroll bar to move to the right date

4 Or press Ctrl+G to launch the Go To Date dialog then carry out the appropriate procedures on the facing page

Inserting a new appointment in the Month Calendar

| Hit Ctrl+N

5 Click here   3 Enter a description

Labels help to classify appointments. Click in the Labels field on the right and allocate one.

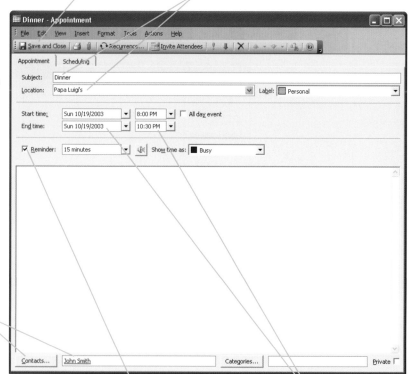

Click Contacts and select an appointee.

Categorize items so you can locate them easily. Click the Categories button and check one or more categories in the dialog that launches.

Create your own category: type – just enter a name in the "Item(s) belonging to these categories" box and select Add to List.

4 Check Reminder and insert a reminder interval if you want Outlook to prompt you when an appointment is due

2 Type in start/end dates and times

Inserting a new event in the Monthly Calendar

| Carry out steps 1–3 on page 148

Working with the Tasks folder

Use the Tasks folder to enter and track tasks. When you've entered a task into the Tasks folder, it also displays in Outlook Today.

Entering a task

If you need to amend or update an existing task, double-click it then change the dialog contents.

Various task views are available in step 2. If you select a more advanced view such as By Person Responsible, you can't use this method to create tasks. Instead, hit Ctrl+N and complete the dialog.

1 In the Navigation Pane, hit Tasks

2 Select Simple List

4 Optionally, type in a due date

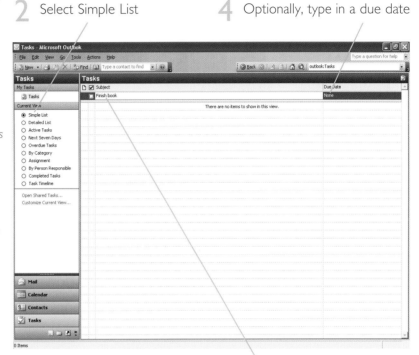

3 Type in a task description

Tasks can be prioritized – there are three levels: Low, Normal (the default) and High. To set a priority, click in the Priority field and select one in the list.

5 Hit Enter

6 To customize the task's settings in more depth (for instance, you can set start and end dates, reminder intervals and/or priority levels), double-click it after step 5. Complete the dialog which launches, then click Save and Close

Working with the Contacts folder

Use the Contacts folder as a convenient place to keep track of business/personal contacts.

Outlook displays contacts in various forms. The two main aspects are as a grid or using a business card model. Another view (Detailed Address Cards) uses the card model but has more detail.

Entering a contact

1 Click Contacts in the Navigation Pane

2 In any view, hit Ctrl+N

Hit Ctrl+Shift+B to view your Address Book.

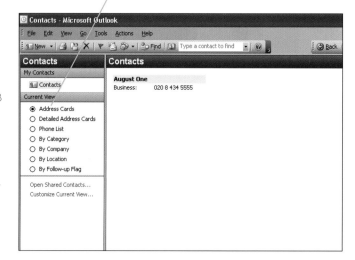

If you need to amend a contact, double-click it. Then carry out steps 3 thru 4 as appropriate.

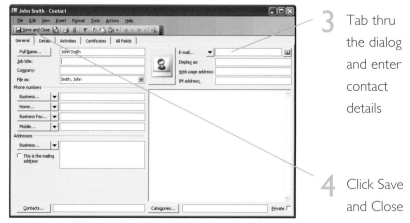

3 Tab thru the dialog and enter contact details

4 Click Save and Close

Composing email

To add a new account after startup, choose Tools, Options. Select the Mail Setup tab and then click E-mail Accounts. Complete the wizard. (To select an account before sending an email, click the Accounts button in the toolbar.)

When you first launch it, Outlook runs a special wizard. Among other things, this specifies which email service options you use and sets these up as a new "account" (it may offer to import a previous account, if applicable). There are two main choices. You can opt to connect via a phone line or by a local area network (LAN). This book assumes you're using the phone-line method exclusively; if you're using the second, consult your system administrator.

After completing the wizard, you should have no difficulty in carrying out the instructions given here and later.

Composing email

To use Word 2003 as your email editor, choose Tools, Options. Select the Mail Format tab and check "Use Microsoft Office Word 2003 to edit email messages". Click OK. Hitting Ctrl+N now launches a new email in a customized version of Word.

1 In the Navigation Pane, hit Mail

2 Hit Ctrl+N

6 Click Send

3 Type in the email address (addresses are completed from email already sent)

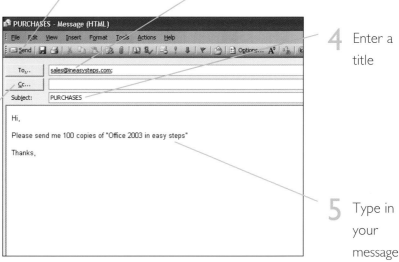

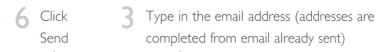

4 Enter a title

5 Type in your message

Want to send the email to more than one contact? Enter their details in the Cc field.

Composing a long email? Hit Ctrl+S to store it temporarily in your Drafts folder.

7 Mail which you've written but which hasn't yet been sent is lodged in the Outbox folder

8 Despatched mail is lodged in the Sent Items folder

Reading and replying to email

Reading email

Once email has been downloaded to you, you can read it in two ways. Do ONE of the following:

You can also have the Reading Pane display at the bottom of the screen (View, Reading Pane, Bottom) or hide it (View, Reading Pane, Off).

2 Double-click a message and read it in the editor which launches

Hit F7 to spell-check your email.

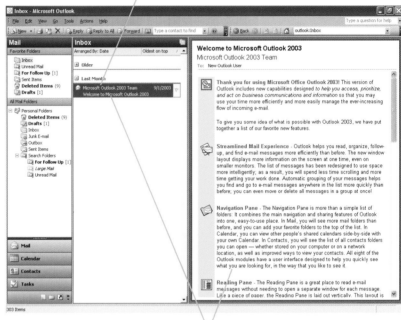

Click an email and read it in the Reading Pane

Replying to email

Here, Outlook 2003 will either launch its own email editor or (if you've followed the procedure in the HOT TIP on page 155) Word 2003 will launch instead.

1 View an email in the Reading Pane or in the separate editor

2 Hit Reply or Reply to All (if the original email was addressed to more than one person and you want to reply to them all)

3 Type in your reply at the head of the email then click Send

Sending/receiving email

To send messages or replies you've composed (and receive any email waiting for you on your ISP's server), do the following from within any of the email related folders:

Every so often, you should "clean up" your Mailbox. Pull down the Tools menu and select Mailbox Cleanup. Complete the Mailbox Cleanup dialog and click OK.

Click Send/Receive (or just hit F9)

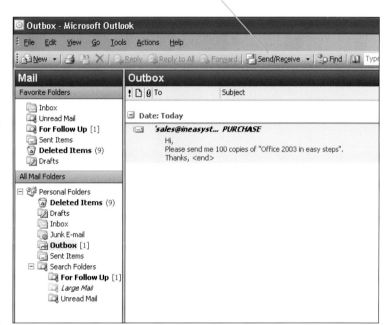

As you can see, you can also view mail in a kind of "mini preview" – just select View, AutoPreview.

You can combat spam by setting up appropriate rules – these perform specified actions on junk mail, like moving it to a folder or deleting it. In the Mail pane, choose Tools, Rules and Alerts. Hit New Rule then work thru the Rules Wizard.

You can also use the Wizard simply to flag messages according to criteria. These include importance, sensitivity or text content.

Outlook 2003 connects to your ISP, sends your email and downloads any waiting for you. Finally, it closes your connection

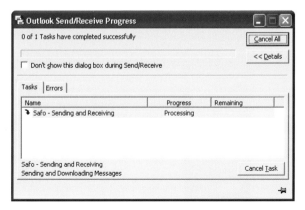

Surfing the Internet

Viewing Web pages directly

I With your Internet connection live, refer to the Web toolbar
(View, Toolbars, Web)

2 Type in a Web address then press Enter

Want to look up data on the Web? When you're reading or composing an email, choose Tools, Research. See page 80 for more information.

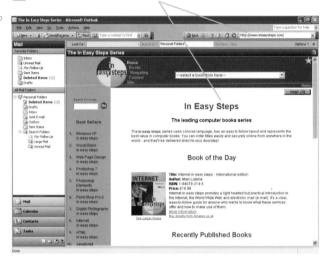

Sending Web pages in email

I After you've carried out step I above, pull down the Actions
menu and click Send Web Page by E-Mail

2 Compose your email then click Send

If Word is your email editor, the Web page appears as an attachment.

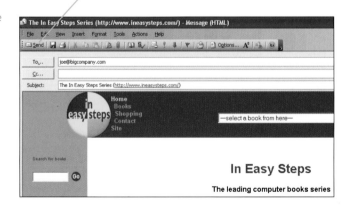

PowerPoint 2003

Here, you'll produce your own professional-quality slide show. You'll automate its creation and then customize it. You'll add/format text; use Smart Tags; work with slide views; insert pictures, diagrams, movies, sounds, animations and hyperlinks; work with slide masters; and apply new design templates/color schemes. Finally, you'll print out your presentation and run it.

Covers

Chapter Five

The PowerPoint 2003 screen

Below is a detailed illustration of the PowerPoint 2003 screen:

Clicking a slide's entry in the Outline/Slide Pane displays it in the Slide area.

You can enter speaker notes into Notes view. Click in it and type in text.

When you've finished, click back in the Slide area.

Title bar   Menu bar   Rulers

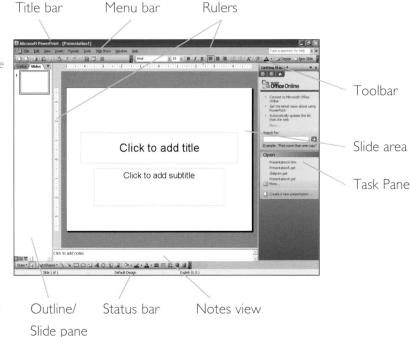

Toolbar

Slide area

Task Pane

Outline/
Slide pane

Status bar

Notes view

Some of these components can be hidden, if required.

Specifying which screen components display

Pull down the Tools menu and click Options. Then:

1 Ensure the View tab is active

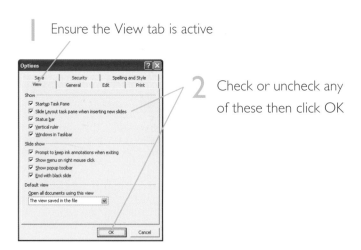

2 Check or uncheck any of these then click OK

The AutoContent Wizard

In Chapter 1, we looked at how to create new Office documents based on templates and Wizards. PowerPoint 2003 has a unique and particularly detailed Wizard which handles the basics of creating a presentation.

Creating a slide show via the AutoContent Wizard

1 In the Getting Started Task Pane, click Create a new presentation

To launch the Task Pane, hit Ctrl+F1.

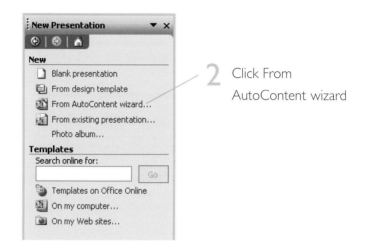

2 Click From AutoContent wizard

3 Complete the Wizard. Below, we're selecting a presentation type

PowerPoint presentations don't just run onscreen: you can also opt to create Web and various kinds of overhead presentations.

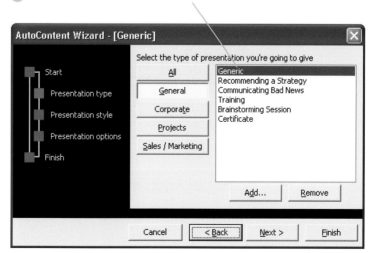

The slide views – an overview

PowerPoint's principal views

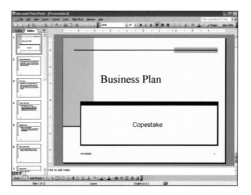

Normal view – displays each slide individually

There are also various master views – see pages 171–172.

Another view – Print Preview – lets you check your presentation before printing it. Hit Ctrl+F2 to launch or close Print Preview.

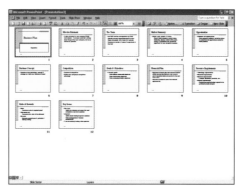

Slide Sorter view – shows all the slides as icons so you can work with them more easily

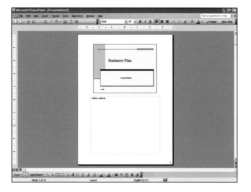

Notes Page view – shows each slide plus any speaker notes

Switching to a view

Pull down the View menu and click the relevant view entry

Normal view also has important subsidiary views.

Secondary views

1 If the Outline/Slide page isn't visible in Normal view, choose View, Normal (Restore Panes)

2 Click the appropriate tab

3 Slide view – shows thumbnails for each slide

4 Outline view – shows the textual structure underlying slides

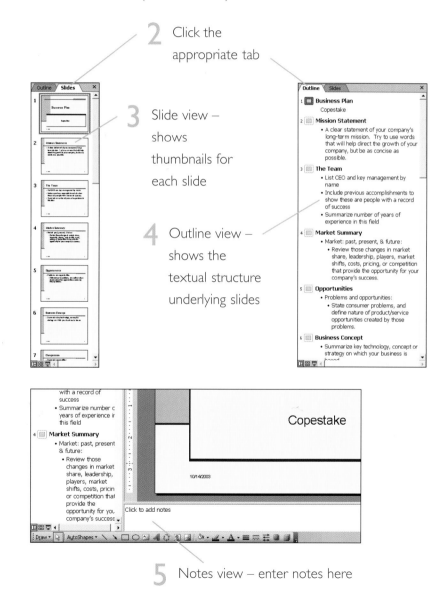

5 Notes view – enter notes here

Using the slide views

All the views have their own default magnification. You can adjust this, however. Pull down the View menu and click Zoom. Select a new percentage and click OK.

(In Print Preview, click in the toolbar Zoom field and select a new percentage.)

The following are some brief supplementary notes on how best to use the PowerPoint 2003 views.

Normal view

Normal view displays the current slide in its own window. Use Normal view when you want a detailed picture of a slide (for instance, when you amend any of the slide contents, or when you change the overall formatting).

You can also use Normal view to:

- work with text. The Outline component of the Outline/Slide pane (see page 160) displays only text. You can amend this text and watch your changes take effect in the Slide area on the right

- enter notes. Simply click in the Notes view below the Slide area and enter speaker note text. (You can also do this within Notes Page view – see below)

To switch from slide to slide, you can press Page Up or Page Down as appropriate. (For more information on how to move around in presentations, see "Moving through presentations" on page 174.)

Slide Sorter view

You can also use Slide Sorter view to perform additional operations – for instance, you can use it to apply a new slide layout to more than one slide at a time.

If you need to rearrange the order of slides, use Slide Sorter view. You can simply click on a slide and drag it to a new location (to move more than one slide, hold down one Ctrl key as you click them, then release the key and drag). You can also copy a slide by holding down Ctrl as you drag.

Notes Page view

You can print speaker notes – see step 9 on page 184.

This view is an aid to the presenter rather than the viewer of the slide show. If you want to enter speaker notes on a slide (for later printing), use Notes Page view.

In Notes Page view, the slide is displayed at a reduced size at the top of the page. Below this is a standard PowerPoint 2003 text object. For how to enter notes in this, see the "Adding text to slides" topic on page 167.

Using grids

You can add a grid to slides within Normal or Notes Page views. This is a useful feature because you can align objects such as pictures to it.

Enabling the grid

In Normal or Notes Page view, pull down the View menu and select Grid and Guides

Ensure Snap objects to grid is checked to have objects "attracted" to the grid.

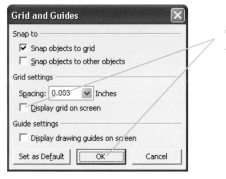

2 Ensure Display grid on screen is checked then confirm

You can also apply manual ("drawing") guides. Ensure "Display drawing guides on screen" is checked. When you close the dialog, I horizontal and I vertical line appear on-screen; drag these to a new location and align objects with them.

The grid structure

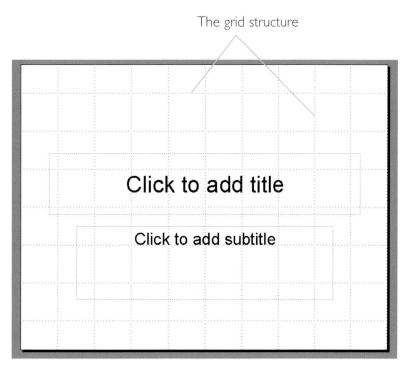

Customizing slide structure

The easiest way to customize the basic format of a slide is to use preset layouts. There are almost 30 of these under various headings (Text, Content, Text and Content and Other). You can apply layouts to one or more slides. When you've done this, you can then amend the individual components (see later topics).

Using preset layouts

Make sure you're in Normal or Slide Sorter view. If you're in Slide Sorter view, Ctrl-click the slide(s) you want to amend. Pull down the Format menu and click Slide Layout.

You can also use the Slide component of the Outline/Slide pane to select multiple slides. Ctrl-click to select thumbnails.

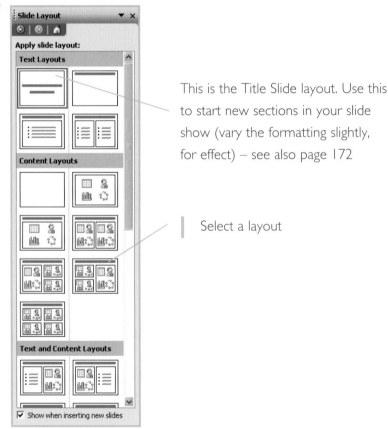

This is the Title Slide layout. Use this to start new sections in your slide show (vary the formatting slightly, for effect) – see also page 172

Select a layout

2 Any slide components present before you applied the new format will still remain but they may need to be resized/moved

Adding text to slides

When you create a new slide show, PowerPoint 2003 fills each slide with placeholders containing sample text. The idea is that you should replace this with your own text.

When you type in text, certain errors are automatically corrected. For example:

- *the first letter in sentences is capitalized*
- *day names are capitalized*
- *specific errors are corrected (e.g. "abbout" becomes "about")*

All these generate AutoCorrect action buttons. Clicking the blue box under the substitution produces a menu; select the appropriate option.

1 Click in a placeholder

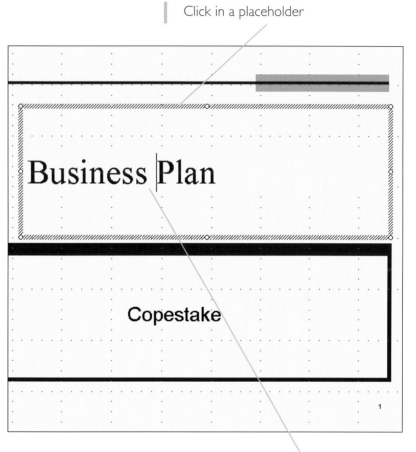

2 PowerPoint displays a text entry box – type in your own text

3 Click anywhere outside the placeholder to confirm the addition of the new text

4 Alternatively, click this button in the Drawing toolbar: then drag out a text box anywhere on a slide. Insert the necessary text

Formatting text

Font-based formatting

1 Click inside the relevant text object and select the text you want to format

2 Pull down the Format menu and click Font then carry out any of steps 3–8 below, as appropriate. Finally, follow step 9:

You can replace fonts globally. Choose Format, Replace Fonts. Specify the old and new font and hit Replace.

3 Select a typeface

4 Type in a new point size

9 Click here

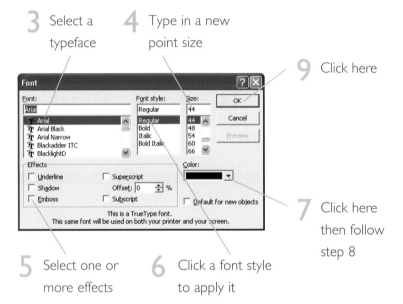

5 Select one or more effects

6 Click a font style to apply it

7 Click here then follow step 8

8 Click a color. If none are suitable, click More Colors and select one in the new dialog

Changing text alignment

1 Click inside the relevant text object and select the text whose alignment you want to amend

2 Pull down the Format menu and click Alignment. In the submenu, select an alignment

Changing text spacing

1 Click inside the relevant text object and select the text whose spacing you want to amend

2 Pull down the Format menu and click Line Spacing

To spell-check text, hit F7. Or, for on-the-fly checking, choose Tools, Options, select the Spelling and Style tab and check "Check spelling as you type".

3 Type in a line spacing

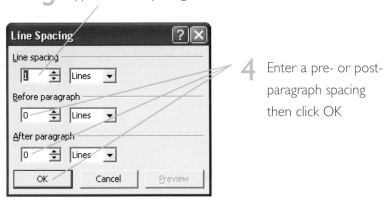

4 Enter a pre- or post-paragraph spacing then click OK

You can also find synonyms, translate text and carry out research on the Net, all from the Research Task Pane. See page 129 for how to do this.

Summarizing slides

You can collect slide titles and insert them into a new slide.

1 In Slide Sorter view, select the slides you want to include then click this toolbar button:

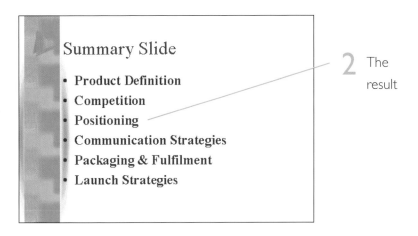

Summary Slide

- **Product Definition**
- **Competition**
- **Positioning**
- **Communication Strategies**
- **Packaging & Fulfilment**
- **Launch Strategies**

2 The result

Color schemes & design templates

Applying a new color scheme or design template is a quick and effective way to give a presentation a new and consistent look.

Any PowerPoint presentation (apart from a blank one) has various color schemes/design templates available to it.

Imposing a color scheme/design template

| Pull down the Format menu and click Slide Design

You can manually apply background fills to slides. Choose Format, Background. Click in the Background Fill box and select a plain color. You can also apply a gradient, pattern or texture fill: just select Fill Effects.

2 Click Design Templates or Color Schemes

Hit Apply to Selected Slides instead if you pre-selected slides.

3 Right-click a template or scheme then select Apply to All Slides

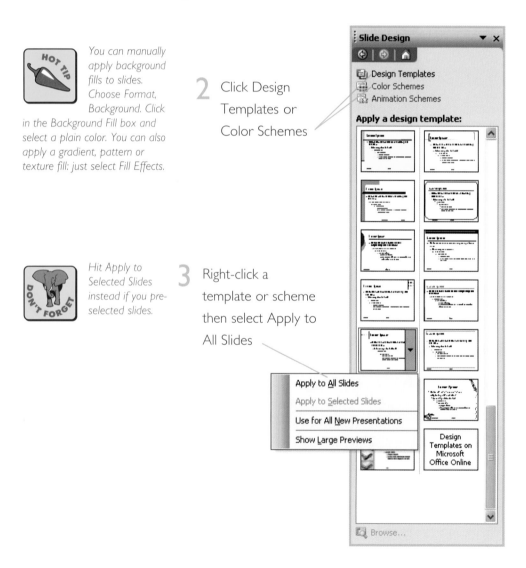

Slide masters

When you apply a design template, PowerPoint automatically adds a "slide master" to your presentation. The idea of slide masters is that you can change or add an element and have this automatically reflected in all the associated slides.

Typical uses for slide masters include:

PowerPoint 2003 slide shows can have multiple slide masters. If you find this feature confusing, you can disable it. Choose Tools, Options. Hit the Edit tab and check Multiple masters.

- inserting pictures (e.g. logos) which you want to appear on all slides

- implementing font formatting which you want to appear on all slides

Editing slide masters

> Pull down the View menu and click Master, Slide Master

You can apply new designs to masters. In the thumbnails on the left of Slide Master view, Ctrl-click the masters you want to change. Now follow the procedures on the facing page (the menu wording is slightly different).

2 Edit the master – e.g. by reformatting text (you can't change the text itself) or (as here) adding pictures

Title masters

Most slide masters are associated with title masters. Use title masters to adjust slides using a title slide layout (see also page 166).

You can "preserve" a master, so it can't be deleted by PowerPoint when all associated slides are erased. Right-click its thumbnail on the left of Slide Master view and choose Preserve Master.

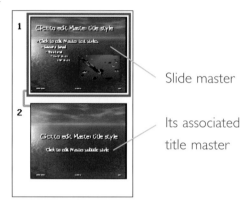

Slide master

Its associated title master

Handouts often accompany presentations. To customize handouts, choose View, Master, Handout Master. Edit any of the placeholders or customize the background (right-click the background and select Handout Background). Or use the toolbar to specify the number of handouts per page.

Notes masters

You can also customize how notes are presented by using the Notes master.

Pull down the View menu and click Master, Notes Master

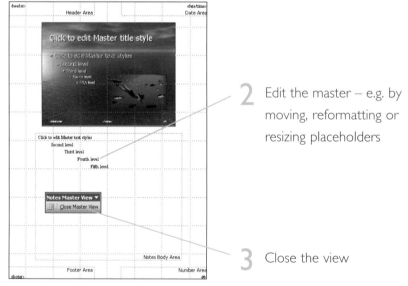

Changes you make to a master only affect those slides that follow it. So you may have to insert objects on more than one master to ensure blanket coverage.

2 Edit the master – e.g. by moving, reformatting or resizing placeholders

3 Close the view

Format Painter

You can use a shortcut (the Format Painter) to copy a color scheme from one presentation to one or more slides in another.

Copying color schemes

You can use Format Painter to copy formatting between text. Format Painter can also copy any formatting you've applied to a picture (e.g. a border) to another image.

1 With both presentations open in Normal view, pull down the Window menu and click Arrange All

2 Carry out step 3 below. In step 4, single-click for one copy or double-click for multiple copies (and see the HOT TIP)

To copy the formatting to more than one slide, double-click in step 4. In step 5, click as many icons as required. When you've finished, press Esc.

4 In the Standard toolbar, click or double-click the Format Painter icon:

3 Click the icon for the slide whose scheme you want to copy

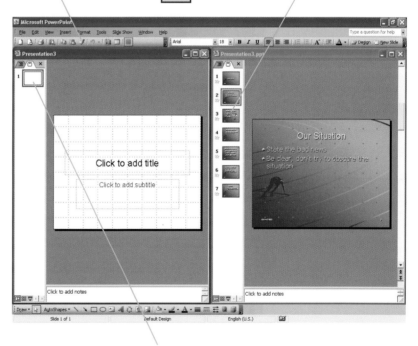

5 Click the icon representing the slide you want to format

6 The new color scheme is now available in the target presentation's Slide Design Task Pane

Moving through presentations

For help with how to move thru presentations when you're actually running them, see page 187.

Since presentations always have more than one slide, it's essential to be able to move from slide to slide easily (it's even more essential in the case of especially large presentations). There are two main methods you can use to do this.

Using the vertical scroll bar

In Normal or Notes Page views, move the mouse pointer over the vertical scroll box. Hold down the left mouse button and drag the box up or down. As you do so, PowerPoint 2003 displays a message box giving you the number and title of the slide you're up to.

PowerPoint lets you broadcast slide shows over Intranets. For help with any aspect of slide show broadcasting (inc. scheduling the broadcast via Outlook), see your system administrator.

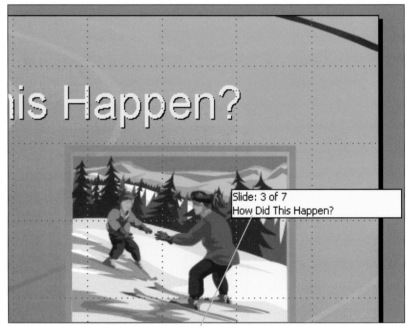

Slide number indicator – when the correct number displays, release the mouse button to jump to that slide

Using Slide Sorter view

Slide Sorter view offers a useful shortcut which you can use to jump immediately to a specific slide. Simply double-click any slide icon within Slide Sorter view; PowerPoint then switches to Slide view and displays the slide you selected.

Smart Tags

By default, Smart Tags are disabled in PowerPoint. To turn them on, choose Tools, AutoCorrect Options. Select the Smart Tags tab and check "Label text with smart tags". Click OK.

PowerPoint 2003 recognizes certain types of text and flags them with a purple dotted underline. When you move the mouse pointer over the line, an "action button" appears that provides access to commands which would otherwise have to be accessed from menus/toolbars or even other programs.

There are several types of Smart Tag in PowerPoint 2003. These include names from your Outlook Contact list or from email recipients and financial symbols.

Using Smart Tags

You can search for and download more Smart Tags from the Web. Choose Tools, AutoCorrect Options. Select the Smart Tags tab and check More Smart Tags. Follow the on-screen instructions.

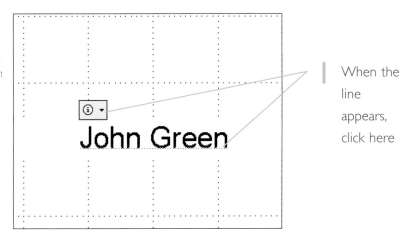

When the line appears, click here

PowerPoint also gives access to extra action buttons that resemble Smart Tags. These are:

- *Paste Options – controls pasted items*
- *AutoCorrect – controls automatic corrections (see also the DON'T FORGET tip on page 167)*
- *AutoFit – controls text resizing to fit placeholders*
- *Automatic Layout – controls slide relaying after you insert pictures etc.*

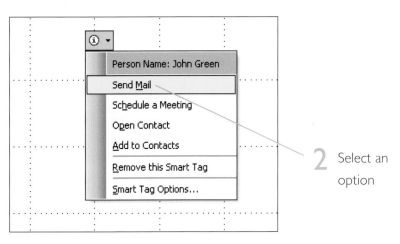

2 Select an option

Inserting and deleting slides

You'll often want to insert a new slide into presentations.

Inserting a slide

1 In Normal or Notes Page view, move to the slide you want to precede the new one. In Slide Sorter view, click the relevant slide

2 Hit Ctrl+M

To delete a slide, pull down the Edit menu and click Delete Slide. The slide and its contents are erased immediately; you can, however, undo the deletion (Ctrl+Z).

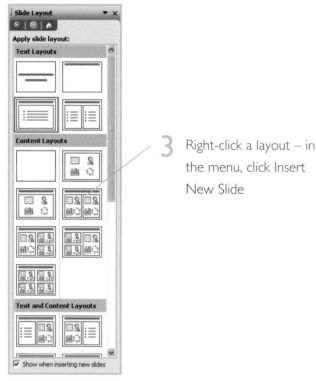

3 Right-click a layout – in the menu, click Insert New Slide

Inserting a slide from another presentation

1 In Normal or Notes Page views, move to the slide that you want to precede the new one

2 Pull down the Insert menu and click Slides from Files. Complete the dialog and click Insert

Inserting pictures

Inserting pictures via the Clip Art Task Pane

In Normal or Notes Page views, go to the slide into which you want the clip art added. Pull down the Insert menu and click Picture, Clip Art. Now carry out the following steps:

To have a picture appear on every slide, add it to the slide master (see pages 171–172). However, if you only want it to appear on most slides, select the ones you want to exclude in Slide Sorter view then choose Format, Background. Check "Omit background graphics from master" then hit Apply.

To add new clips to collections (or add new keywords to existing clips), click the Organize clips link at the base of the Task Pane.

You can also add pictures via a dialog. Choose Insert, Picture, From File then complete the dialog.

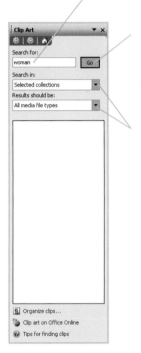

1. Enter one or more keywords (these help you find clips)

3. Click Go

2. Optional – click here and make the appropriate choices

4. Click an icon to insert the clip

5. Want more clips? Click Clip art on Office Online for access to a wide variety (and a lot more besides)

Inserting movies and sounds

1 In Normal or Notes Page views, go to the slide into which you want the movie or sound added

2 Ensure your Internet connection is live (for access to more movies or sounds)

3 Pull down the Insert menu and click Movies and Sounds. Select Movie from Clip Organizer or Sound from Clip Organizer

You can add movies and sounds from files, too. Just select Movie from File or Sound from File in the submenu then complete the dialog.

PowerPoint now supports lots of new file types with new features (for instance, you can play video full screen by right-clicking the movie, selecting Edit Movie Object and then clicking Zoom to full screen). These formats include Advanced Stream Redirector (.asx), Windows Media Redirector (.wvx) and Windows Media Audio Redirector (.wma).

If the required codec isn't installed on your system, PowerPoint and Media Player should download it automatically.

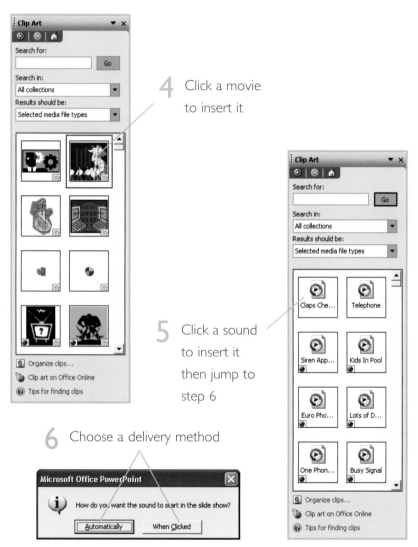

4 Click a movie to insert it

5 Click a sound to insert it then jump to step 6

6 Choose a delivery method

Playing tracks from audio CDs

You can play tracks from audio CDs during a presentation.

Inserting CD tracks

In Normal or Notes Page views, go to the slide into which you want the audio track added and choose Insert, Movies and Sounds, Play CD Audio Track

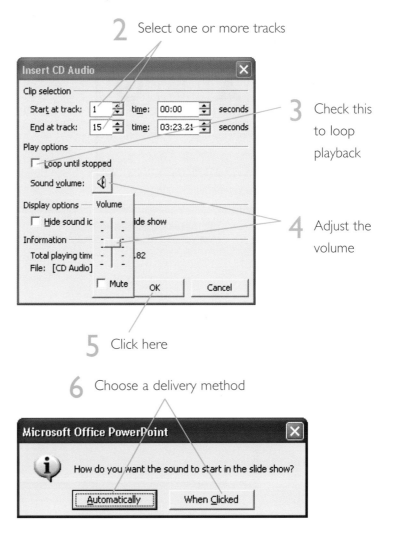

2 Select one or more tracks

3 Check this to loop playback

4 Adjust the volume

5 Click here

6 Choose a delivery method

Inserting diagrams

You can insert diagrams (e.g. pyramids and org charts) into slides.

I In Normal or Notes Page view, pull down the Insert menu and click Diagram

You can also use the diagramming tools on the Drawing toolbar (View, Toolbars, Drawing) to create diagrams.

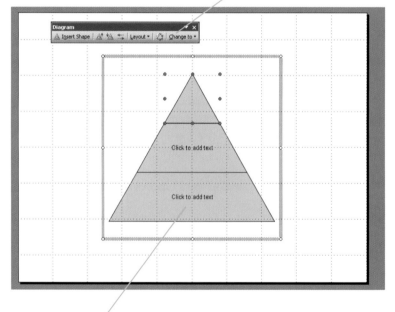

2 Select a diagram then hit OK

4 Make any further changes e.g. click "Change to" to convert to another diagram or "Layout" to make layout changes

To create flowcharts, use AutoShapes. Click AutoShapes on the Drawing toolbar then use the Flowchart, Lines and Connectors options.

3 An inserted pyramid – edit it as required e.g. click a text placeholder and type in text, or resize it

Inserting animations

You can apply animations to slides. In PowerPoint, animations are defined as visual/sound effects applied to text and/or objects. You can apply standard animation schemes (often the best idea) or you can apply customized effects to specific objects.

Applying an animation scheme

1 Optionally, go to Slide Sorter view and select the slides you want to animate

2 Pull down the Slide Show menu and click Animation Schemes

PowerPoint 2003 has new animation effects, all available from the Slide Design Task Pane. However, you can disable these if you find that your system's performance suffers. Choose Tools, Options. Go to the View tab and check New animation effects in the Disable new features section.

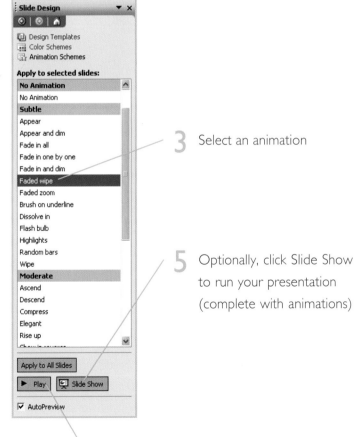

3 Select an animation

5 Optionally, click Slide Show to run your presentation (complete with animations)

Click Apply to All Slides if you want the animation added to the whole slide show.

4 Optionally, run the animation – watch the slides update

Customizing animations

1 Go to the relevant slide in Normal view and click the object you want to animate

2 Pull down the Slide Show menu and click Custom Animation

You can add more than one animation to any given item.

3 Click the Add Effect button. In the menu, select a category; in the submenu, select an effect

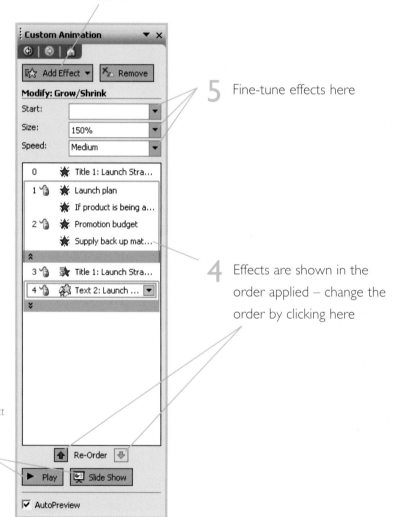

5 Fine-tune effects here

4 Effects are shown in the order applied – change the order by clicking here

Preview the effect you've created or run your presentation:

Inserting hyperlinks

You can insert hyperlinks into slides. In PowerPoint, hyperlinks are "action buttons" which you can click (while a presentation is being run) to jump to a destination. This can include a specific slide, a URL, another slide show or another file.

Inserting an action button

1 In Normal or Notes Page view, pull down the Slide Show menu and click Action Buttons. In the submenu, select a button

2 On the slide, drag to define the button

3 Click here

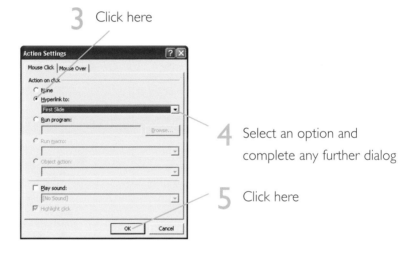

4 Select an option and complete any further dialog

5 Click here

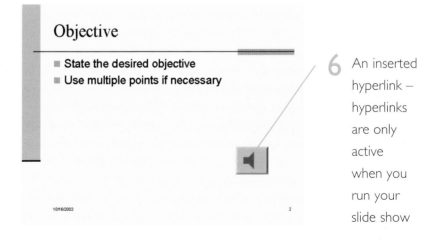

6 An inserted hyperlink – hyperlinks are only active when you run your slide show

Printing

Printing a presentation

1 Choose File, Page Setup

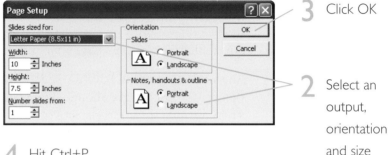

3 Click OK

2 Select an output, orientation and size

4 Hit Ctrl+P

5 Click here; select a printer

6 Click here to print the current slide only

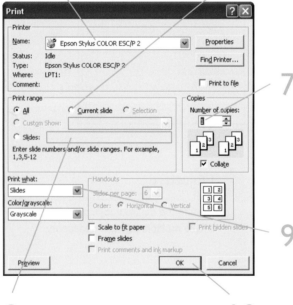

7 Type in the number of copies required

9 Click here; select a presentation component

8 Type in a range – e.g. to print slides 2, 5 and 9 type in "2,5,9". To print slides 2 to 7, type in "2-7" (omit all quotes)

10 Click here

Running a presentation

Once you've created (and possibly printed) your slide show, it's time to run it. Before you do so, however, you should set the run parameters.

When you run your presentation you can, if you want, have PowerPoint 2003 wait for your command before moving from slide to slide. This is useful if you anticipate being interrupted during the presentation. You retain full control over delivery.

Alternatively, you can have the slide show run automatically. Before you can do this, though, you have to set various parameters. These include the intervals between slides, which slides you want to run and the presentation type.

Preparing to run your slide show

First, open the presentation you want to run. Then pull down the Slide Show menu and click Set Up Show. Now do the following:

1 Select a slide show type (normally Presented by a speaker)

2 If you don't want all the slides to run, enter start and end slide numbers

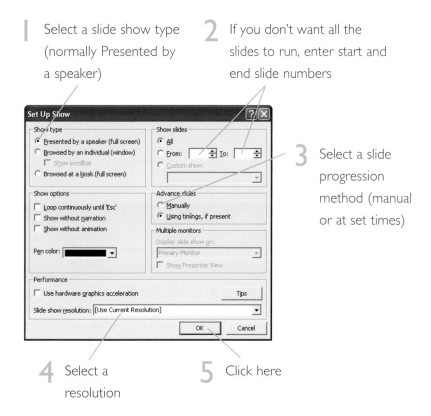

3 Select a slide progression method (manual or at set times)

4 Select a resolution

5 Click here

Running a manual presentation

Pull down the Slide Show menu and click View Show. If you selected Manually in step 3 on page 185, PowerPoint runs the first slide of your presentation and pauses. When you're ready to move on to the next slide, left-click once or press Page Down. If you need to go back to the previous slide, simply press Page Up as often as required.

Running an automatic presentation

Before you can run an automatic presentation, you have to set the slide intervals. You can do this by "rehearsing" the slide show.

Stage 1

Pull down the Slide Show menu and click Rehearse Timings, then do the following:

If you want to end your slide show at any time, simply press Esc. This applies to manual and automatic presentations.

If you didn't opt for automatic playback, you'll have to click movie, sound and CD track icons to play them while you're giving the presentation.

You can also run your slide show on another computer, even one that lacks PowerPoint. The only requirements are that it should be running Windows 98 SE or later and have a CD drive.

Pull down the File menu and click Package for CD – this launches the Package for CD dialog. Hit Options to specify exactly what's involved in the copying process. Complete the rest of the dialog then hit Copy to CD.

When the recipient inserts the CD into the drive, the slide show runs automatically.

1 This timer counts the interval until the next slide; when the timing is right, follow step 2

2 Click here & repeat steps 1–2 for all the slides

Rehearsal ▼ ✕
⇨ ❙❙ 0:00:10 ↺ 0:00:10

3 Click here when all the slides have been allocated times

Microsoft Office PowerPoint ✕

(i) The total time for the slide show was 0:00:07. Do you want to keep the new slide timings to use when you view the slide show?

Yes   No

Stage 2

After rehearsal, pull down the Slide Show menu and click View Show. If you clicked "Using timings, if present" in step 3 on page 185, PowerPoint 2003 displays the first slide and moves on to subsequent slides after the rehearsed intervals have elapsed.

PowerPoint 2003 now has a dedicated toolbar you can use to help you present your slide show. The Slide Show toolbar is unobtrusive, even subtle, so it won't be obvious to your audience yet it provides access to the features you'll use most often.

Using the Slide Show toolbar

When you're running the presentation, rest the mouse on the slide to display the toolbar

If the toolbar is elusive, make sure it's enabled. Choose Tools, Options. Select the View tab and check Show popup toolbar.

Use the toolbar arrows to step back and forward thru the slides.

When you run a slide show, PowerPoint displays an arrow as a pointer – it's hidden after 3 seconds of inactivity and reappears when you move the mouse. To display the arrow all the time, follow step 2 then select Arrow Options followed by Visible.

Or select another pointer option like Felt Tip Pen or Highlighter – use these to emphasize screen contents.

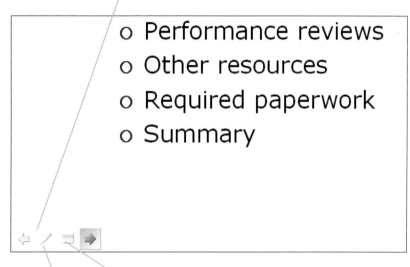

o **Performance reviews**

o **Other resources**

o **Required paperwork**

o **Summary**

2 Click here to produce this menu:

| Arrow |
| Ballpoint Pen |
| Felt Tip Pen |
| Highlighter |
| Ink Color ▶ |
| Eraser |
| Erase All Ink on Slide |
| Arrow Options ▶ |

3 Click here to produce this menu:

| Next |
| Previous |
| Last Viewed |
| Go to Slide ▶ |
| Custom Show ▶ |
| Screen ▶ |
| Help |
| Pause |
| End Show |

Running presentations in Explorer

Presentations display authentically in Internet Explorer (especially if you're using version 4 or above). You can even run presentations from within Internet Explorer.

This means that slide shows converted to HTML format and saved to the Web can be run by the majority of Internet users.

Running slide shows in Internet Explorer

1 Open a HTML version of a presentation in Internet Explorer

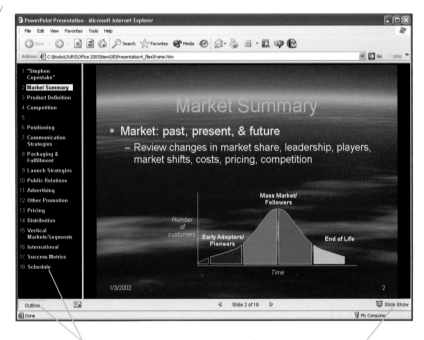

2 Click Outline to hide or unhide the slide outline

3 Click Slide Show to run your show in Full-Screen mode

To halt the slide show before the end, press Esc.

4 Internet Explorer now launches the first slide so that it occupies the whole screen. When the last slide has been reached, a special screen displays with the following text:

End of slide show, click to exit.

5 Click anywhere to return to Internet Explorer's main screen

Access 2003

This chapter will rapidly get you up-and-running with Access. First you'll get to grips with basic techniques like creating and navigating thru databases and generating new tables and forms. Then you'll format your tables and forms, add new labels/fields (including Smart Tags), error-check and search for data. Finally, you'll create reports and charts, customize database layout then preview and print your work.

Chapter Six

Covers

The Access 2003 screen

Below is a detailed illustration of a typical Access 2003 screen:

This is Datasheet view, one of several ways of viewing and interacting with your data.

Menu bar   Toolbar

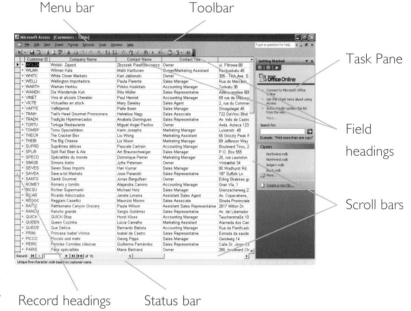

Task Pane

Field headings

Scroll bars

Backup your databases regularly, before you make any major changes. Choose File, Back Up Database. Complete the dialog.

Record headings   Status bar

Specifying whether specific components display

Pull down the Tools menu and click Options. Then do the following:

Ensure the View tab is active

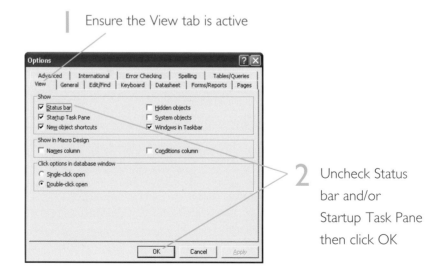

2 Uncheck Status bar and/or Startup Task Pane then click OK

Basic database terminology

Before you can learn to use Access 2003 to create databases, you need to be familiar with and understand the following terms:

Database	Information grouped together (and organized for ease of reference) into an Access file
Tables	Used to store data in rows/columns
Records	(Horizontal) rows of data in tables. Each record is a complete set of related data items
Fields	(Vertical) columns of data in tables. Fields are spaces reserved for specified data

Fields

		Product ID	Product Name
▶	+	1	Chai
	+	2	Chang
	+	3	Aniseed Syrup
	+	4	Chef Anton's Cajun Seasoning
	+	5	Chef Anton's Gumbo Mix
	+	6	Grandma's Boysenberry Spread
	+	7	Uncle Bob's Organic Dried Pears
	+	8	Northwoods Cranberry Sauce

A table excerpt

Records

A further component – reports – displays table data in a customized format (with page numbers and headings). Reports can't be edited, but they can contain data from one or more tables.

Forms	Use forms to display table data in a customized format. Forms display one record at a time and are often the most convenient way to interact with data. Below is a sample form:

Tables, forms and reports are all "objects" and can be selected/ manipulated.

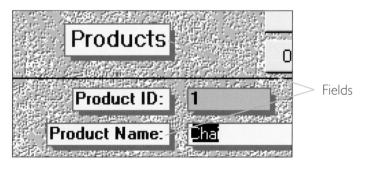

Products

Fields

Product ID: 1

Product Name: Chai

Automating database creation

Before you start to create a database, it's a good idea to plan it out first, even if only roughly. Pre-planning can take various forms.

First, study how your data is currently organized and use this as a base. Second, be sure about the categories into which data can be split logically. Third, plan out which fields you need.

Pre-planning also involves determining which fields within specific tables can serve as "primary keys". The primary key is the field which is common to each record and which identifies it as being unique. Primary keys are also used to determine the order in which records are sorted.

1 To create a database with the help of a Database Wizard, pull down the File menu and click New

2 In the Task Pane, click On my computer...

3 Select the Databases tab

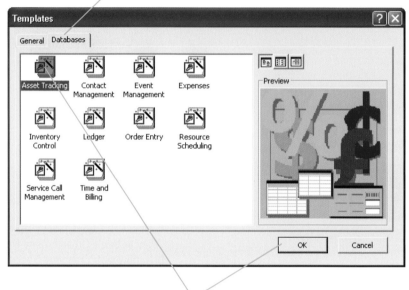

4 Select a template and confirm

5 Use the File New Database dialog to name and save your database and click Create

6 Work thru the remaining Wizard dialogs. You'll:

- specify the fields contained within tables
- apply a screen style
- apply a report style
- name the database
- (optionally) include a picture

The Database window

When you create a new database in Access 2003 (or open an existing one), the Database window displays. Since this is the basis for table creation, we need to discuss this before we move on.

1 If the Database window isn't visible, press F11

You can't do much to customize the Database window. What you can do, though, is:

- *specify how objects display (e.g. with small or large icons) – click the relevant toolbar icon*

- *specify the order of objects on the right – select View, Arrange Icons then an option*

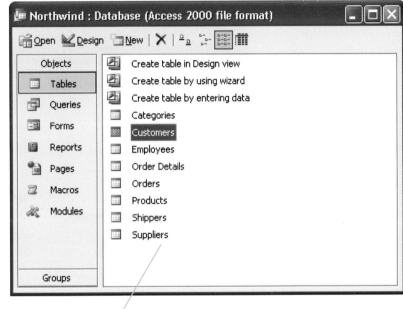

2 The Database window

Don't want to display the Database window at startup? Choose Tools, Startup and uncheck Display Database Window.

3 Periodically, hit F5 to refresh the Database window (especially in multi-user environments)

The Database window can be thought of as a command center for the active database. For example, clicking on the Close button closes the database. It's also the basis from which much of the work you carry out with tables, forms and reports is undertaken.

Automating table creation

To create a table manually, select "Create table by entering data" in step 2 then amend the table design.

1 Hit F11 if the Database window isn't visible

2 In the Database window, select the Tables tab on the left then double-click "Create table by using wizard" on the right

3 Choose a table category

5 Double-click the field(s) you want to include – they appear on the right

Data in tables is organized into columns ("fields") and rows ("records").

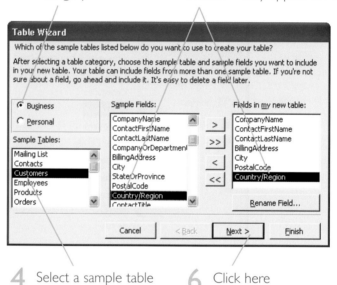

4 Select a sample table

6 Click here

7 Type in a name for your table

A further dialog (concerned with relationships between tables) may appear after this one. Access may decide that your new table is related to other tables in your database i.e. they have records in common. It's usually safe to accept the defaults but, if necessary, you can click Relationships and define the relationships yourself.

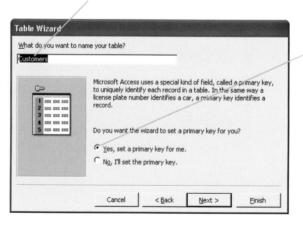

8 Opt to let Access set a primary key (often the best idea)

...cont'd

9 Select an option here – if you want to enter data straightaway, select either of the lower two options

You can create tables from imported data. With the Database window active, choose File, Get External Data, Import. Double-click the Access file you want to import from. In the new dialog, select the Tables tab and double-click a table – Access adds it to the Database window.

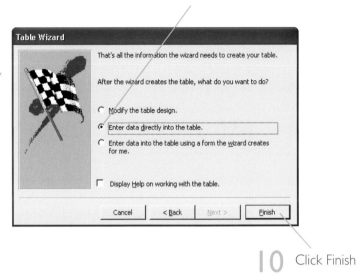

10 Click Finish

11 If you selected "Enter data into the table using a form..." in step 9, start filling out the form

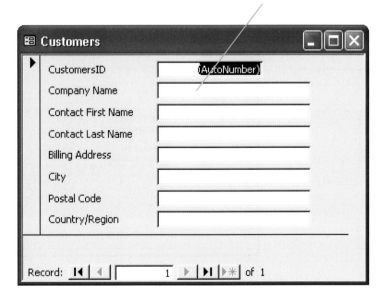

Amending table design

1 If the table is already open, chose View, Design View

2 If the table isn't already open, hit F11 and follow steps 3–4

3 Select Tables on the left of the Database window

When you close the Design View window, you're prompted to save your work.

4 On the right of the Database window, right-click the table you want to amend and select Design View in the shortcut menu

5 Either way, the Design View window appears:

Field Format pane

The key symbol denotes the primary key.

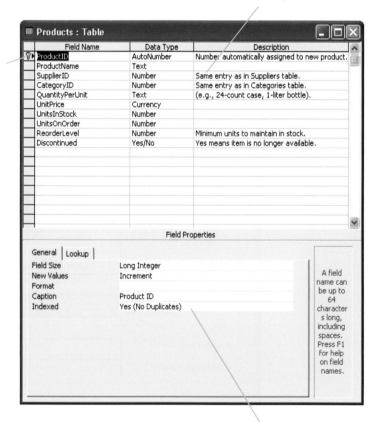

Field Properties pane

Setting up new table fields

| Enter Design View – see the facing page

3 Click here

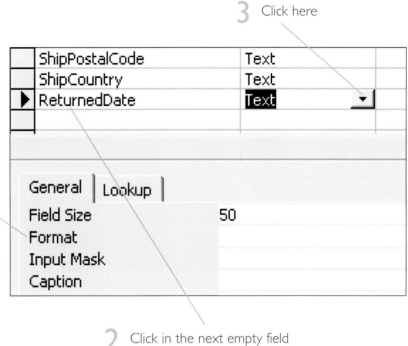

	ShipPostalCode	Text	
	ShipCountry	Text	
▶	ReturnedDate	Text	▼

General | Lookup |

Field Size   50
Format
Input Mask
Caption

Some fields (like Format) may be linked ("bound") to controls in forms and reports. When you change the properties of such fields, Access displays an action button. You can opt to cascade the effect to the bound controls or you can select "Help on propagating field properties" for more assistance.

2 Click in the next empty field and name the new field

Text
Memo
Number
Date/Time
Currency
AutoNumber
Yes/No
OLE Object
Hyperlink
Lookup Wizard...

4 Select a data type – AutoNumber (it enters a unique ID reference automatically) usually needs no reformatting

5 For more on data types, see overleaf

Every Access field must have a data type – it determines what kind of data it can hold. Data types in Access strongly resemble data types in Excel – for example, common instances are Date/Time, Currency and Text.

For more on a specific data type, select it in the Design View window then press F1.

Points to bear in mind when allocating data types

1 You need to consider the type of value you want to store. Although you can store numbers in a field with a Text data type, the converse isn't true

2 You also need to consider the types of operations you'll need. For instance, you can't tell Access to add up Text values . . .

3 Take account, too, of the way you want to sort values within fields. Sorting is an integral part of database use but it may not be clear how this applies to data types. For example, on the face of it Access will sort numerical values in a Text data type without any problems. The reality, though, is that it will sort them, not as numbers, but as text strings. Date values also do not sort well in a Text or Memo data type

4 What's the difference between the Text and Memo data types? The following should help:

- Use the Text data type to store any data (including numerals like phone and social security numbers) that don't require calculation. A Text field can store up to 255 characters
- Use the Memo data type to store 256 thru 65,536 characters

5 Storage space is another factor to pay attention to. You should consider the amount you want to use for values in any given field

Forms – an overview

Once you've created an Access 2003 database (and possibly one or more tables to go with it), you likely will want to create forms to view your data in a more "user-friendly" way. If you used a Database Wizard to create your database, you'll already have one or more tailor-made forms ready to use (even then, however, you may well want to create your own). If, on the other hand, you created the database manually, you'll have to create any forms you need. The procedures outlined here apply to both scenarios.

Using AutoForm

AutoForm produces simplified forms based on existing tables.

You can import forms (and also tables, reports and other Access components)
from other Access databases. From the Database window, pull down the File menu and click Get External Data, Import. Locate the Access file then select the components you want to import.

1 In the Database window, activate the Tables tab on the left then double-click a table

2 In the Table Datasheet toolbar, click the arrow next to:

3 In the menu, select AutoForm

4 The AutoForm appears – all fields and records in the base table display, and each field appears on a separate line:

Forms can sometimes take unusual forms, such as dialog boxes or "switchboard" forms.

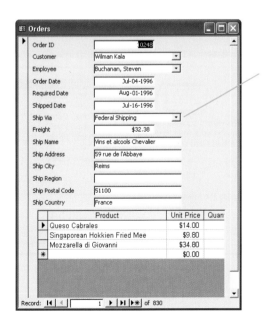

5 Enter data – use AutoForms when you want to create a form based on a single table

Automating form creation

Use the Form Wizard when you want to create a form based on more than one table.

> If the Database window isn't visible, hit F11

To open a form, double-click it in the Database window.

3 Click New

2 Activate the Forms tab

To create a form manually, carry out steps 1–3. Select Design View in step 4 then select a base table in the same dialog. Click OK. Access creates the new form in Design view (with easy access to fields in the selected table).

You can also create AutoForms: select AutoForm: Columnar or AutoForm: Tabular. In both cases, select a table or query then hit OK.

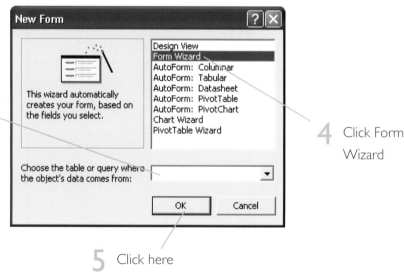

4 Click Form Wizard

5 Click here

...cont'd

Access 2003 now launches the Form Wizard. Carry out the following steps:

If you want to use fields from additional tables or queries, repeat steps 6 thru 7.

6 Click here; select a base table or query in the list

7 Double-click the field(s) you want to include

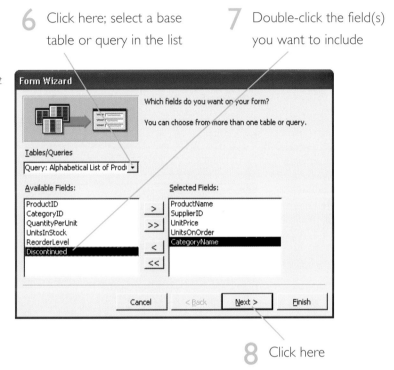

8 Click here

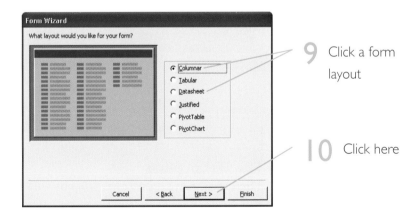

9 Click a form layout

10 Click here

11 Complete the remaining wizard screens (select a style and name the form) then click Finish to create the form

Amending form design

1 If the form is already open, chose View, Design View

2 If the form isn't already open, select Forms on the left of the Database window. Right-click the form you want to redesign and select Design View in the menu

3 Either way, Access launches the form in Design View:

5 Add a new field by dragging it from the Field List onto the Detail pane or header/footer

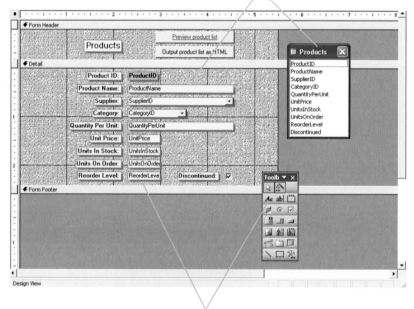

4 Add a new element (e.g. a label) by selecting its icon and dragging on the Detail pane or header/footer

The Detail pane

The Detail pane represents the current body of your form. Here, you create and design the necessary fields.

| To resize the Detail pane (or any other element), drag an edge or corner outwards or inwards

Troubleshooting the Field List

Access 2003 has Smart Tags, but they're implemented in a different way.
Right-click a field in any form in Design View and select Properties. In the dialog, select the Data tab. Click in the Smart Tags field and select a Tag.

Make sure Smart Tags are enabled. Choose Tools, Options. Select the Forms/ Reports tab and check "Show Smart Tags on Forms".

Access also gives access to extra action buttons that resemble Smart Tags. These include Paste Options and AutoCorrect – see page 36 for more information.

The new field will likely be called "Field1". To give it a meaningful name, right-click the new column just after it's been created – in the menu, select Rename Column. Overtype a name then hit Enter.

The Field List has no fields

1 If no fields appear in the Field list, right-click the Detail pane and select Properties in the menu

2 Select Form then the Data tab

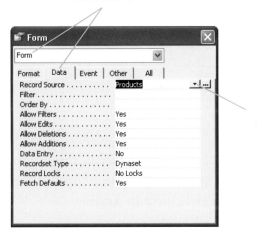

3 Click here in the Record Source field and select a base table or query

How do I get more fields in the Field List?

1 Use the Database window to open the table that underlies the form

2 Click the column to the left of which you want the new column (field) inserted then choose Insert, Column

3 When you reopen the original form, the new field appears in the Field List

Error checking

In forms and reports, you can have Access flag common errors.

Ensuring error checking is enabled

1 Choose Tools, Options

2 Select Error Checking

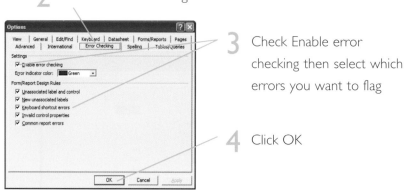

3 Check Enable error checking then select which errors you want to flag

4 Click OK

Error checking in action

1 Here, selecting two unassociated fields produces an action button

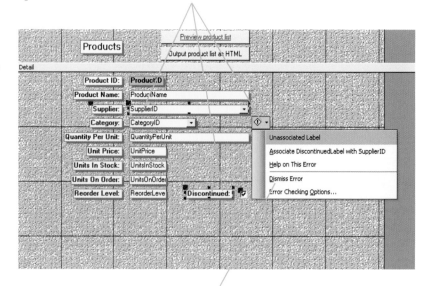

For how to use Smart Tags, see page 203.

2 Make the appropriate choice in the menu

Entering data

1 To create a new record in Datasheet or Form view, press Ctrl++

To insert the Euro symbol – € – into an Access 2003 field, hold down Alt and press "0128" (minus the quotes) on the numerical keypad to the right of your keyboard. Finally, release Alt.

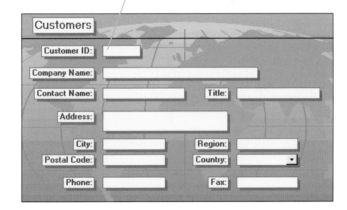

+	WANDK	Die Wandernde Kuh	Rita Müller
+	WARTH	Wartian Herkku	Pirkko Koskitalo
+	WELLI	Wellington Importadora	Paula Parente
+	WHITC	White Clover Markets	Karl Jablonski
+	WILMK	Wilman Kala	Matti Karttunen
+	WOLZA	Wolski Zajazd	Zbyszek Piestrzeniewicz

A new record in Datasheet view

2 The new record

A new record in Form view

To cancel amendments you've made to the active field, press Esc.

3 Type in the necessary data and press Enter (the insertion point moves to the next field)

4 Repeat step 3 as necessary

5 If you don't want to enter data in a given field, press Enter or Tab (or Shift+Tab to reverse the direction) as often as necessary until the insertion point is in the correct field

6 When you jump to another record, Access automatically saves your amendments

Amending data

To edit existing database data, click the appropriate field in the relevant record (this applies to both Datasheet and Form views). One of two things happens now:

- if the field is empty, you can begin typing in data immediately

- if the field already contains data, Access highlights it. Simply begin typing and overwrite the existing data

Using the Zoom box

The Zoom box is, in effect, a special editing window which displays the whole of a field's contents, however extensive.

The next illustration shows the field detail section of an address field in a database form:

Brecon House
Fifth Floor

The address here consists of three lines, but only two display in the form. To view and/or edit the entire field, click in it. Then press Shift+F2. Now carry out the following steps:

Type in replacement data, or click outside the highlighted text and make any necessary revisions

You can use the Zoom box in Form and Datasheet views.

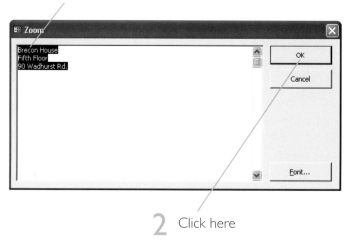

2 Click here

Database navigation

Using the Record Gauge
Press F5 to activate the Record Gauge. Then click as appropriate:

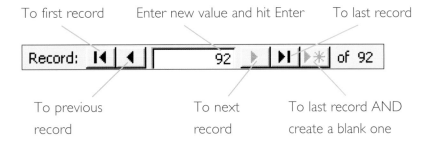

To first record   Enter new value and hit Enter   To last record

Record: 92 of 92

To previous record   To next record   To last record AND create a blank one

Using keyboard shortcuts

In Datasheet view, you can use the scroll bars to move to other records. In Form view, however, scroll bars move you to hidden areas of the current record.

The following keystroke combinations can be used to move around in both Datasheet and Form views:

End	Moves to the last field in the record
Home	Moves to the first field in the record
Ctrl+End	Moves to the last field in the last record
Ctrl+Home	Moves to the first field in the first record
↑	(In Datasheet view and tables only) goes to the active field in the previous record
↓	(In Datasheet view and tables only) goes to the active field in the next record
Ctrl+ ↑	Moves to the active field in the first record
Ctrl+ ↓	Moves to the active field in the last record
Page Up	Moves up by one screen
Page Down	Moves down by one screen
Ctrl+Page Up	(In Datasheet view) Moves one screen to the left
Ctrl+Page Down	(In Datasheet view) Moves one screen to the right

In Form view, Page Up and Page Down move to the previous or next record, respectively, when the start or end of the current record has been reached.

In Form view, Ctrl+Page Up takes you to the previous record, and Ctrl+Page Down to the next.

Spell-checking data

Spell-checking a form or table

1 Open a form or table

2 In the case of data in Datasheet view, select the record(s), column(s), field(s) or text you want to check. In the case of Form view, select the field or text you want to check

3 Hit F7

4 If one of the suggestions here is correct, click it, then follow step 5

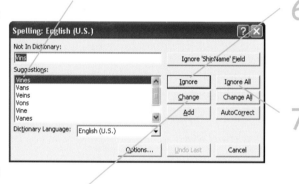

6 Click Ignore to ignore just this instance

7 Click Ignore All to ignore all future instances

5 Click Change to replace this instance

Additional options

8 The column being checked appears in the Ignore... field at the top of the dialog; click this to stop Access from checking this column

9 Click AutoCorrect to add the incorrect word (together with your correction) to AutoCorrect; now Access will correct the word for you automatically

10 Click Add to have the flagged word stored in CUSTOM.DIC or click Change All to have Access substitute its suggestion for all future instances of the word

Saving to the Web – an overview

You can save database objects – in a variant of HTML or in XML format – to network, Web or FTP servers.

HTML

When you export HTML files in Access 2003 they can be viewed directly from within Internet Explorer 5.x or later with no appreciable loss of data or formatting.

XML

You can also publish Access data on the Web in Extensible Markup Language (.XML) format, which specializes in describing/distributing data. Whereas HTML concentrates on describing how Web pages look, XML specifies how Web data is structured. How it's presented is the subject of a presentation file (called a "schema") which means that any application reading the XML data can present it in a host of different ways.

Another advantage of XML is that it's platform-independent: it can be utilized across the Internet, by different computers and applications.

Types of Web saving

Access 2003 lets you work with several different types of Web page. These include:

Dynamic HTML

Dynamic HTML files are also known as "server-generated" files and display as a table in any browser. To create a dynamic HTML file, output any table or form to ASP (Active Server Pages) format.

Use dynamic HTML for data which changes frequently and in any browser.

Static HTML

You can export any table, form or report to static HTML. In browsers, exported reports display as reports while tables and forms display in Datasheet view.

Use static HTML if you don't have access to the latest version of browsers or your data is not likely to be updated frequently and you don't want to interact with it.

To import HTML or XML data, pull down the File menu and click Get External Data, Import. In the Import dialog, locate and select the relevant data file. Click OK. Complete the dialog(s).

XML is the de facto language for data structuring and delivery on the Web. It's a data-interchange format in that it specializes in exchanging data between dissimilar platforms and software.

You can import XML data too – from the Database window, choose File, Get External Data, Import. During import, the transform file is applied automatically.

Saving to static HTML

Exporting database components

1 In the Database window, activate the Tables, Forms or Queries tab on the left then double-click a table or form on the right

2 If you only want to export a portion of a table, pre-select it

3 Pull down the File menu and click Export

4 Click here and select a recipient

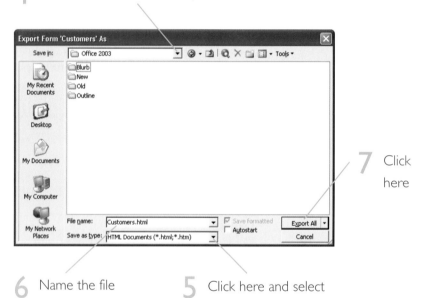

7 Click here

Check AutoStart to view the exported file in your browser.

6 Name the file

5 Click here and select HTML Documents...

8 Ensure Save formatted is selected to save your HTML file in a format which resembles Datasheet view

9 If "Save formatted" was selected (see step 8) Access 2003 launches a special dialog. Click OK to create your HTML file with a default format

10 Publish your file to the Web

Saving to XML

Export your data to XML if you want to reopen it in Excel.

1 Follow steps 1–4 on the facing page

2 In step 5 on the facing page, select XML (.xml)

3 Follow steps 6–7 on the facing page

4 Specify what to export

8 Click here

5 Optional – click here for more options (e.g. if your data is live)

6 If you followed step 5, select a tab and make the relevant changes. For example, activate Data and specify what to export and where the file is saved. Or select Schema, choose whether to include a primary key and name the output (.xsd) file

When you specify a transform file during export to XML, the transform is applied automatically.

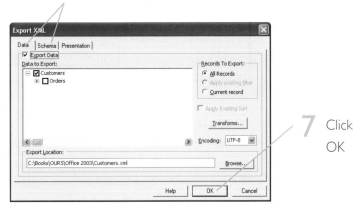

7 Click OK

Saving/publishing to dynamic HTML

You can't export reports to dynamic HTML.

1 Follow steps 1–4 on page 210

2 In step 5 on page 210, select Microsoft Active Server Pages (*.asp). You can also select Microsoft IIS 1-2 (*.htx; *.idc)

There are differences between ASP and IDC – for more information, see your system administrator.

3 Perform steps 6–7 on page 210

4 Complete these options, as appropriate – in particular, enter:

- the location of a HTML template
- a Data Source Name
- a user-level security username and password in the "User to Connect As" and "Password for User" fields

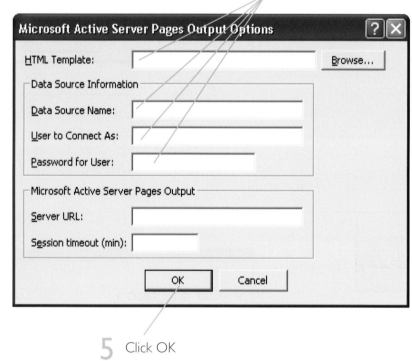

The instructions here are guidelines to the overall procedure. Consult your system administrator for more specific information.

5 Click OK

6 Publish your files to the Web

Find operations

Access 2003 lets you search the active database for text and/or numbers. You can:

- search through all fields within every record, or limit the search to a specific field in every record

- search forwards or backwards, or through the whole database

- limit the search to exact matches (i.e. Access 2003 will only flag data which has the same upper- and lowercase make-up). For instance, a case-specific search for "man" will not flag "Man" or "MAN"

To restrict the search to a specific field in every record, select the field before you launch the Edit menu then select it in step 2.

- limit the search to "match types" (the beginning of fields, the whole field or any part) – see step 4 below

Searching for data

Pull down the Edit menu and click Find. Carry out step 1 below, then steps 2–4, as appropriate. (Additionally, see the HOT TIPS for other ways to customize the search.) Finally, carry out step 5:

Re step 1 – you can also enter wildcards. "?" stands for any one character while "" stands for any number of characters (omit the quotes).*

For case-specific searches, check Match Case.

1 Type in the data you want to find

2 Click here; select a field or datasheet/form to search

5 Click here to flag the next match

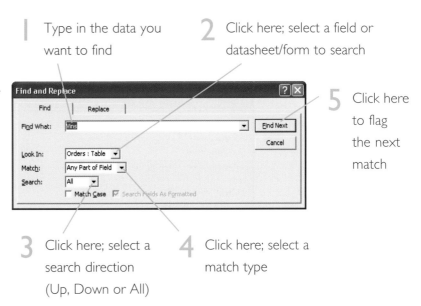

3 Click here; select a search direction (Up, Down or All)

4 Click here; select a match type

Repeat step 5 as necessary to locate further instances of the data specified in step 1.

Find-and-replace operations

When you search for data you can also have Access 2003 replace it with something else. You can:

- search through all fields within every record, or limit the search to a specific field in every record

- search forwards or backwards, or through the whole database

- limit the search to exact matches (i.e. Access 2003 will only flag data which has the same upper- and lowercase make-up)

If you want to restrict the search to a specific field in every record, select the field before you launch the Edit menu. Then select it in step 3.

Replacing data

Pull down the Edit menu and click Replace. Perform steps 1–2, then 3–4 if relevant. Now do one of the following:

- Follow step 5. When Access 2003 locates the first search target, carry out step 6 to have it replaced. Repeat as often as required

- Carry out step 7 to have *every* target replaced automatically

1 Type in the data you want to find

2 Type in replacement data

5 Click here to flag the 1st occurrence

To specify a search direction, click in the Search field and select Up, Down or All.

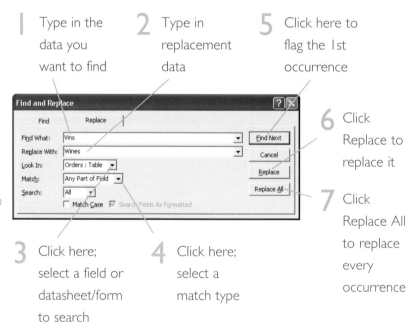

6 Click Replace to replace it

7 Click Replace All to replace every occurrence

3 Click here; select a field or datasheet/form to search

4 Click here; select a match type

Sorting data

Find operations locate records based on one criterion. However, you can also arrange records in a specific order; this is "sorting". Sorting helps you find data more quickly in tables and forms. You can sort data in ascending order (with this level of priority: 0 to 9 then A to Z) or in descending order (9 to 0, Z to A).

Carrying out a sort

In forms and tables in Datasheet view, you can sort by more than one field (from the left, but only in the same sort order). Simply select more than one column before you sort.

1 In either Datasheet or Form view, click the field on which you want to base the sort

2 Pull down the Records menu and click Sort, Sort Ascending or Sort, Sort Descending

You can also perform more complex sorts (for example, with one field Ascending and one Descending). In the dialog on page 216, complete more than one column (Access sorts from the left) in the Design grid but omit the criteria. Choose Filter, Apply Filter/Sort.

Alfreds Futterkisten	Maria Anders
Ana Trujillo Emparedados y helados	Ana Trujillo
Antonio Moreno Taquería	Antonio Moreno
Around the Horn	Thomas Hardy
Berglunds snabbköp	Christina Berglund
Blauer See Delikatessen	Hanna Moos
Blondel père et fils	Frédérique Citeaux
Bólido Comidas preparadas	Martín Sommer
Bon app'	Laurence Lebihan
Bottom-Dollar Markets	Elizabeth Lincoln
B's Beverages	Victoria Ashworth
Cactus Comidas para llevar	Patricio Simpson
Centro comercial Moctezuma	Francisco Chang

Before the sort...

Centro comercial Moctezuma	Francisco Chang
Cactus Comidas para llevar	Patricio Simpson
B's Beverages	Victoria Ashworth
Bottom-Dollar Markets	Elizabeth Lincoln
Bon app'	Laurence Lebihan
Bólido Comidas preparadas	Martín Sommer
Blondel père et fils	Frédérique Citeaux
Blauer See Delikatessen	Hanna Moos
Berglunds snabbköp	Christina Berglund
Around the Horn	Thomas Hardy
Antonio Moreno Taquería	Antonio Moreno
Ana Trujillo Emparedados y helados	Ana Trujillo
Alfreds Futterkisten	Maria Anders

...after a descending sort has been applied to the field on the far left

3 To return your data to the way it was before a sort, choose Records, Remove Filter/Sort

Filtering data

This method produces complex filters. Two simpler methods are:

• *Filter by Selection (you select a value and Access returns matching records)*

• *Filter by Form (a version of the datasheet or form appears and you complete the relevant empty fields to match these)*

Select these from the Records, Filter menu.

Sorting data is one way of customizing the way it displays on screen. Another method you can use is "filtering". When you apply a filter, Access 2003 temporarily hides records which don't match the requirements ("criteria") you set. Filtering involves:

• selecting the fields through which Access 2003 should search

• specifying the sort order

• specifying what the fields must contain (criteria)

• applying the filter

Setting up a filter

1 In Datasheet or Form view, choose Records, Filter, Advanced Filter/Sort

2 Double-click a field to have it appear in the Field box

Repeat steps 1 thru 3 for as many fields as you want to add to the filter.

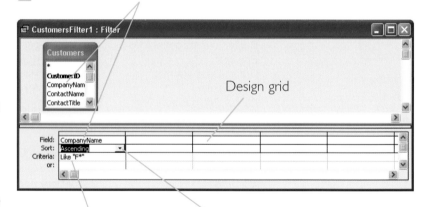

Design grid

Criteria are usually simple to use. For instance, you can use standard wildcards. "B" pulls in all entries beginning with "B", like "Bonus".*

4 Type in criteria in the Criteria field

3 Click the arrow on the right of the Sort field – in the list, select Ascending or Descending

5 Choose Filter, Apply Filter/Sort

6 To remove a filter, choose Filter, Remove Filter/Sort

Querying data

Queries are another way to selectively view data. When you set up and institute a query, you "interrogate" the active database; the result can then be viewed on screen or printed. At the same time, the information which does not satisfy the criteria you implemented is temporarily ignored. You can use a Wizard approach to create a query.

1 If the Database window isn't visible, hit F11

2 Ensure Queries is activated

3 Click the New button

You can base queries on a filter that you've created and saved as a query.

Save your query for reuse (it appears under "Queries" in the Database window). Choose File, Save As and complete the dialog.

To apply an existing query, select "Queries" in the Database window then double-click it.

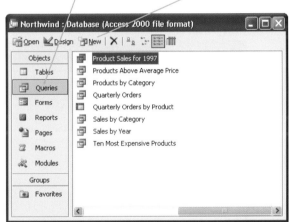

4 In the first Wizard screen, select Simple Query Wizard then complete the remaining screens (select a base table or another query, specify fields then name the query)

5 You can choose to open the query automatically (it displays in Datasheet view)

Reporting

Forms allow you to enter data in a user-friendly way. Reports have a similar effect on the way you view (and print) data. When you create and view a report, however, you have more control over the layout and the ability to customize the printed output. Reports display data in a printed format but don't have to contain all the fields in the base table.

To open a report, double-click its entry in the Database window.

Creating reports via AutoReport

1 If the Database window isn't visible, hit F11

2 Select Reports on the left of the Database window, then New in the toolbar

Before you set up and institute a report, you should carry out the following:

- *examine your database, taking account of the current tables and forms*
- *be clear which components represent data and ensure you've entered all the necessary data*
- *if you want to enter data as well as view it, use a form*
- *review previously created reports with a view to highlighting areas which need improving*

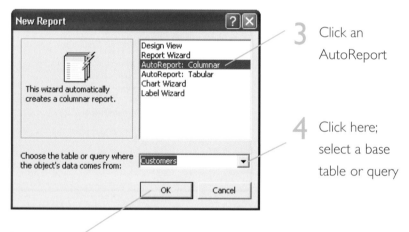

3 Click an AutoReport

4 Click here; select a base table or query

5 Click here – the report uses the last AutoFormat applied (see the DON'T FORGET tip on page 202) or the standard one

In reports created with AutoReport, all fields/records in the base table display and each field appears on a separate line.

6 A columnar report

Using the Report Wizard

1 In the Database window, select Reports on the left then New in the toolbar. Then select Report Wizard and hit OK

2 Double-click the field(s) you want to include

Re step 2 – if you want to use fields from an additional table or query, click the arrow to the right of the Tables/Queries box. Make one or more selections from the list. Finally, double-click the relevant fields and carry out steps 3–5, as appropriate.

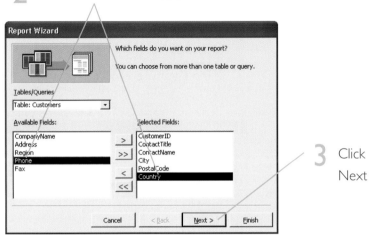

3 Click Next

4 Double-click a heading field (if any of the fields can be grouped under a convenient heading)

To create a report manually, choose Design View in step 3 on the facing page. The report opens in Design view – add labels and fields as for forms (see page 202).

Manually generated reports have to be saved – in Design view, choose File, Save As.

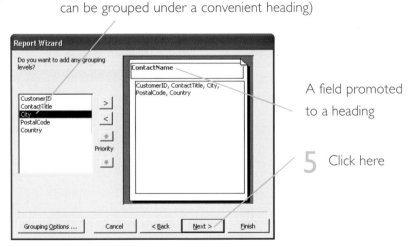

A field promoted to a heading

5 Click here

6 Complete the remaining wizard dialogs (select fields to sort the report by, apply a layout and style and name the report) then click Finish

Creating a graph

First, ensure the Database window is visible. Then carry out the following steps:

Viewing your data visually as a graph can make it easier to take in and absorb.

1   In the Database window, select Reports on the left then New in the toolbar. Then select Chart Wizard

2   In the "Choose a table or query..." field, select a base table or query and hit OK

3   Double-click fields you want to include

To add an existing chart from another file, open a form or report in Design View. In the Toolbox, select this button:

On the form or report, click where you want the chart to appear. In the dialog, select Create from File and use Browse to locate the Access file that contains the chart. Hit OK.

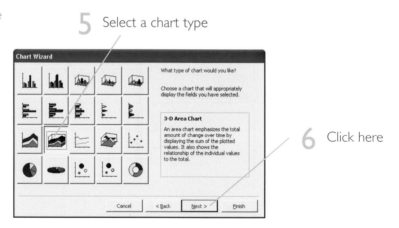

4   Click here

5   Select a chart type

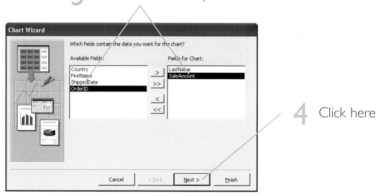

6   Click here

7   Complete the remaining wizard dialogs (select where you want the fields to go and name the chart) then click Finish to generate the graph

Page Setup issues

Page setup settings are stored with forms and reports, so you only have to enter them once for each component. With a table, however, you have to input them each time you want to print it.

Open a table, form or report then choose File, Page Setup

Setting margin sizes

Ensure the Margins tab is active

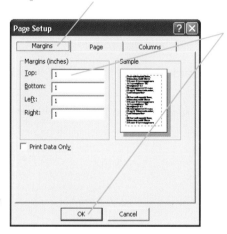

2 Adjust the relevant margin settings and click OK

In tables, ensure Print Headings is ticked to print column headings. (In forms, the field becomes Print Data Only. Check it to ignore gridlines, labels and borders when printing.)

Setting page size/orientation

Ensure the Page tab is active

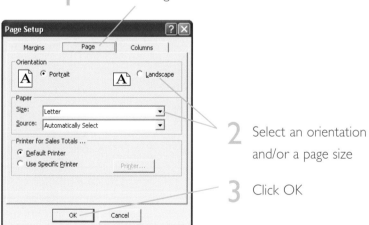

2 Select an orientation and/or a page size

3 Click OK

Specifying column layouts

In forms or reports, you can determine:

If you intend to print tables, forms or reports, you need to ensure that the correct page setup/layout settings are applied.

- how many columns data prints in

- the inter-column spacing

- the column width and/or height

- the gap between rows

- the order in which Access 2003 prints fields within records

1 In the Database window, activate the Forms or Reports tab on the left, then double-click a form or report on the right

2 Choose File, Page Setup

4 Type in the no. of columns

3 Activate the Columns tab

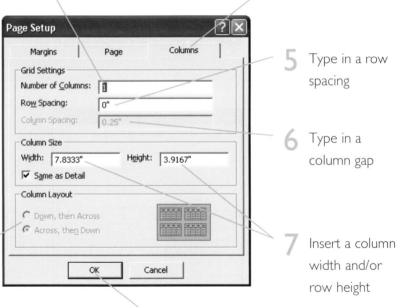

5 Type in a row spacing

6 Type in a column gap

7 Insert a column width and/or row height

Specify print direction in the Column Layout section.

8 Click OK

Using Print Preview

1 To preview a database component, choose File, Print Preview

2 Access 2003 launches a special Print Preview window showing how the component will look when printed:

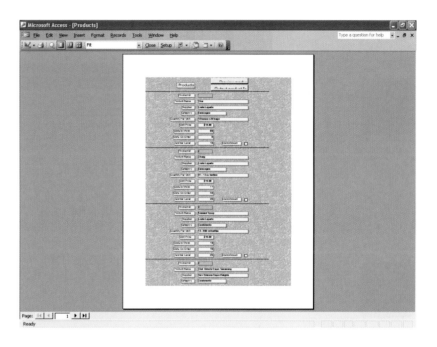

Using the Print Preview toolbar

Select any of the following in the toolbar at the top of the Print Preview screen:

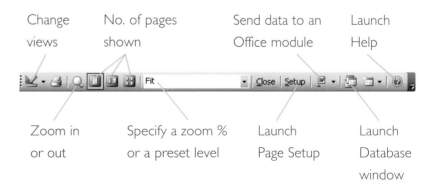

Change views

No. of pages shown

Send data to an Office module

Launch Help

Zoom in or out

Specify a zoom % or a preset level

Launch Page Setup

Launch Database window

Printing your data

1   Preview the component you want to print then hit F11

2   Open a table, form, report or query then hit Ctrl+P

3   Select a printer

4   Uncheck this to turn off collation

5   Type in the no. of copies

If you need to adjust your printer settings, click Properties.

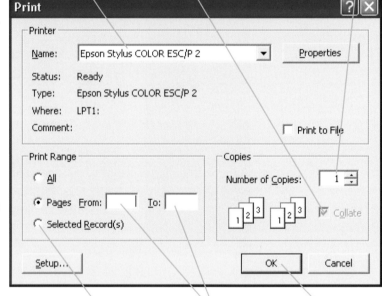

Print

Printer

Name: Epson Stylus COLOR ESC/P 2   Properties

Status: Ready
Type: Epson Stylus COLOR ESC/P 2
Where: LPT1:
Comment:

☐ Print to File

Print Range

○ All
● Pages   From: ☐   To: ☐
○ Selected Record(s)

Copies

Number of Copies: ☐ 1

☑ Collate

Setup...   OK   Cancel

If you print from within a form that is open in Design view, it prints in Form view.

7   Select this to print pre-selected records only

6   Type in start and end page numbers

8   Click here to start printing

9   Alternatively, to print out your data with the current settings applying (a useful shortcut for proofing purposes), just click this icon in the Standard toolbar:

Mail merging

Office's various modules are optimized to work together – in fact, that's precisely what makes Office 2003 so useful. You can create a letter, format it, insert the appropriate fields and then "merge" it with a distribution list (for example, an Access database or your Outlook contacts) to produce a highly tailored result which you can then print and/or edit.

Mail merging can be complex but Word's Mail Merge Wizard makes the whole process easy. You can even use the Wizard to produce mass emailings.

Covers

Chapter Seven

Mail merging – an overview

One of the strengths of the various Office 2003 modules is that they work together very well, and one of the main ways they do this is when you create and run a mail merge.

Mail merging is the process of:

You can also carry out a mail merge from within Access (when you do, Access hooks up with the Word Mail Merge Wizard).

In the Database window, select a table, form or report. Choose Tools, Office Links, Merge It with Microsoft Word and follow the instructions.

1.   creating a "main document" in Word 2003 – this contains the text and/or pictures used in every copy of the final merged document

2.   creating or opening a data source – this contains the information which is absorbed selectively into the main document. Data sources are basically lists of names and addresses

3.   adding merge fields to the main document – these are placeholders. For example, you might have a field called *surname* that pulls in this information from the data source

4.   merging data from the data source into the main document – this creates a new, merged document which is then printed (usually) or edited

Mail merging can be a fairly complex procedure. Luckily, you can use Word's Mail Merge Wizard (based in a special application of the Task Pane) to make it just as effective but much easier and straightforward.

You can also use mail merging to:

- create labels

- create envelopes

- create directories

- create mass email

Mail merging between Word and Access or Excel is a great timesaver.

Running a mail merge

From within a new blank document in Word, pull down the Tools menu and do the following:

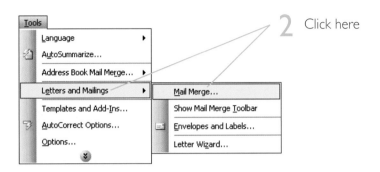

2 Click here

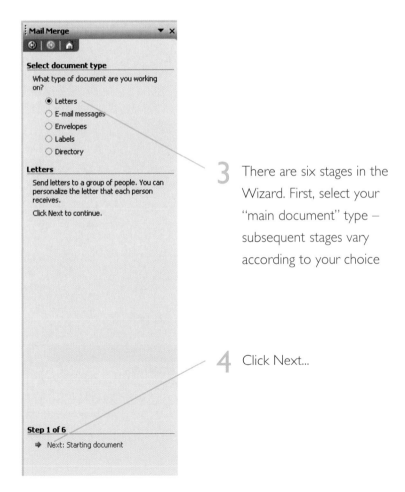

3 There are six stages in the Wizard. First, select your "main document" type – subsequent stages vary according to your choice

4 Click Next...

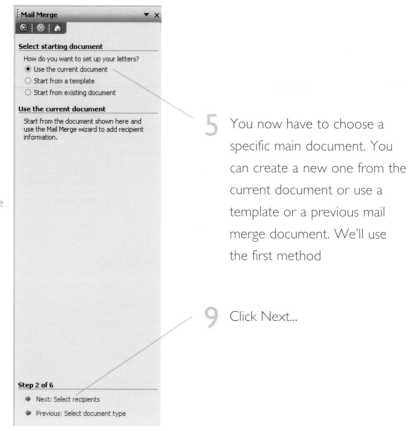

5 You now have to choose a specific main document. You can create a new one from the current document or use a template or a previous mail merge document. We'll use the first method

9 Click Next...

6 If you opted to use a template in step 5, a new link appears. Click Select Template and locate one in the dialog

7 If you opted to use an existing mail merge document in step 5, a new dialog appears:

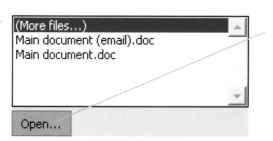

8 Click Open and select a document in the dialog

You can use numerous types of document as a data source. These include Outlook contact lists, Excel workbooks, Access databases, HTML files and text files.

After step 11, two further dialogs appear if (as in this example) you opted to use an Access database as your data source. Select a table in the first. In the second, select/deselect recipients.

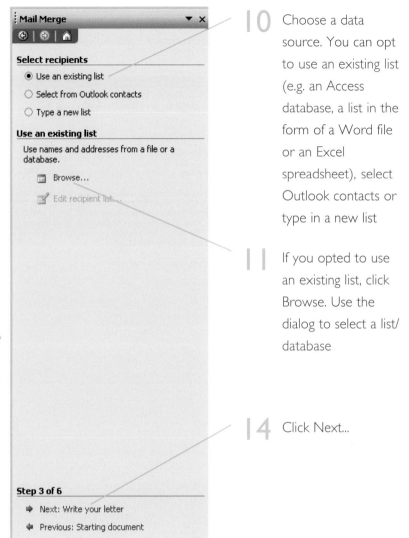

10 Choose a data source. You can opt to use an existing list (e.g. an Access database, a list in the form of a Word file or an Excel spreadsheet), select Outlook contacts or type in a new list

11 If you opted to use an existing list, click Browse. Use the dialog to select a list/database

14 Click Next...

12 If you opted to use Outlook contacts in step 10, click Choose Contacts Folder and follow the onscreen instructions

13 If you opted to create a new list in step 10, click Create... Access launches a form where you can enter contact information

15 It's now time to insert the necessary fields. Click in the appropriate location in your document then select a field type

HOT TIP

Don't want "Dear" or any other salutation to appear? In step 16, select (none) in the Greeting line format box.

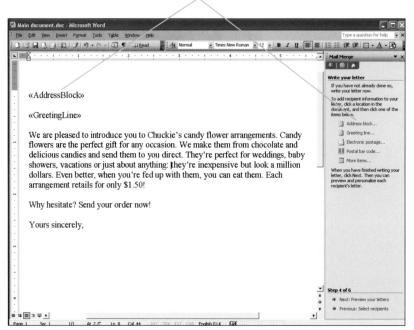

HOT TIP

You may need to format merged data, especially if your data source and main document are formatted differently. In the main document, select the relevant merge field (including the demarcation characters to each side). Press Ctrl+D and complete the dialog.

DON'T FORGET

You can revert mail merge documents to standard Word documents. On the Mail Merge toolbar (View, Toolbars, Mail Merge) click this button:

In the dialog, select Normal Word document.

16 Complete the dialog which launches (this is an example) and click OK

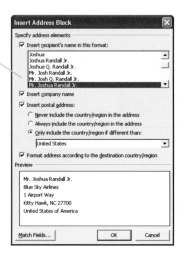

17 In the Task Pane, click Next: Preview your letters

You can view or hide underlying merge codes by hitting Alt+F9.

18 Office merges your document with the selected data source and displays the first merged document:

> Great Lakes Food Market
> 2732 Baker Blvd.
> Eugene 97403
> USA
>
> Dear Sir or Madam,
>
> We are pleased to introduce you to Chuckie's candy flower arrangements. Candy flowers are the perfect gift for any occasion. We make them from chocolate and delicious candies and send them to you direct. They're perfect for weddings, baby showers, vacations or just about anything: they're inexpensive but look a million dollars. Even better, when you're fed up with them, you can eat them. Each arrangement retails for only $1.50!
>
> Why hesitate? Send your order now!
>
> Yours sincerely,

Save your main document, so you can reuse it.

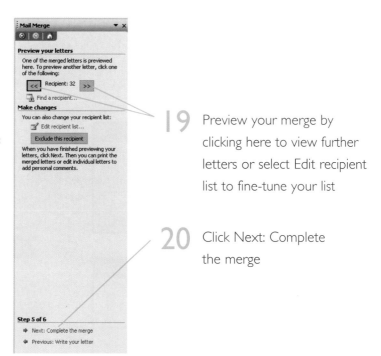

Click Exclude this recipient to omit the current addressee.

19 Preview your merge by clicking here to view further letters or select Edit recipient list to fine-tune your list

20 Click Next: Complete the merge

If, in step 3 on page 227, you selected an option other than Letters, this Task Pane may be different. For instance, if you selected E-mail messages, clicking Electronic Mail in step 21 produces a special dialog where you also specify To:, Subject line: and Mail format: options.

21 Merging is complete – you can send the merge results to your printer. Or you can send them to a new *superdocument* consisting of all the letters created by the merge – you can then edit this as required

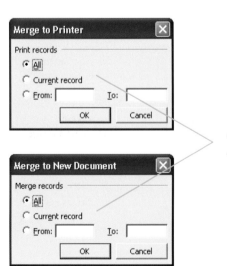

22 Complete the relevant dialog then click OK

Index

P

Q

R

S

T

X